THE AGA KHAN PROGRAM AT THE HARVARD UNIVERSITY GRADUATE SCHOOL OF DESIGN

CAMBRIDGE, MASSACHUSETTS

THE SUPERLATIVE CITY

DUBAI AND THE URBAN CONDITION

IN THE EARLY TWENTY-FIRST CENTURY

EDITED BY **AHMED KANNA**

ISBN 9780977122431

Book and cover design by Wilcox Design | www.wilcoxinc.com
Printed and bound by Kirkwood Printing
Distributed by Harvard University Press

Cover image: Boris Brorman Jensen

The Harvard University Graduate School of Design is a leading center for education, information, and technical expertise on the built environment. Its departments of Architecture, Landscape Architecture, and Urban Planning and Design offer masters and doctoral degree programs and provide the foundation for its Advanced Studies and Executive Education programs.

Illustration credits

Cover, Boris Brorman Jensen; 18, Maksymb; 21, Ministry of Planning and Dubai Municipality; 22, Royal Photographer Noor Ali Rashid; 26, 27, Harris maps courtesy of Mark Harris Architect; 29, Motivate Publishing, copyright 2002; 30, photograph by Peter Rowe; 34–47, all images courtesy Amale Andraos and Dan Wood; 48–61, all photographs by Boris Brorman Jensen; 62, 65, 66, 67, 71, photographs by Charlie Koolhaas; 63, Landsat; 74, 85, Virginie Picon-Lefebvre; 76, *Vogue* magazine; 86, courtesy of Dominique Rouillard, *Le site balnéaire* (Brussels: Mardaga, 1984); 91, 93, 99, diagrams by Neyran Turan; 95, courtesy of TECOM; 104–121, all photographs by Yasser Elsheshtawy; 122–137, all photographs by Ahmed Kanna, except 127 (bottom) and 135 (right), by Ines Hofmann Kanna; 138–147, all photographs by Maryam Monalisa Gharavi; 148–166, all photographs by Kevin Mitchell, except 154 and 158 (*Gulf News*).

CONTENTS

ACKNOWLEDGMENTS

I would like to thank the Aga Khan Program at the Harvard University Graduate School of Design for providing a generous fellowship through which it was possible to initiate this project, and especially to Hashim Sarkis, who along with being a mentor, has been unstinting in his encouragement, support, and, most important, his stimulating intellectual engagement. Thanks also to: Melissa Vaughn, publications director at the GSD; Jean Wilcox, book series graphic designer; the Stanley Foundation of Iowa City and the International Programs at the University of Iowa, for providing travel funds to Dubai; Jane Desmond, Virginia Dominguez, Martha Greer, Vicki Hesli, Bill Reisinger, and Downing Thomas, for generously accommodating me at the International Studies program at the University of Iowa; all my friends and colleagues in Dubai and the UAE, for their patience in helping me decipher their society and culture; George Katodrytis, for his patience and intellectual engagement; Steve Caton, Engseng Ho, and Ted Bestor, who continue be an inspiration; and Xiangming Chen and Vijay Prashad, who recruited me to Trinity College, provided a stimulating environment in which to continue my writing and thinking, and whose engagement has helped open new perspectives on Dubai and many other contemporary cities besides. Above all, I would like to thank the contributors to this volume, who took time from their packed academic and professional schedules to provide insightful chapters. Finally, as always, to my partner, best friend, and wife, Ines: words don't suffice.

AHMED KANNA

1

INTRODUCTION

As relatively recently as the first half of 2008, it was still common among journalists and scholars to refer to Dubai as a paradise of urbanism, an open frontier where all sorts of experiments in free market-capitalism were possible, and as Zaha Hadid's colleague Patrik Schumacher put it, a laboratory for the architectural profession.[1] Yet since the worldwide financial contraction, mass-media representations of the city are almost the opposite. We now often hear about large projects abandoned, expatriates fleeing the city, workers laid off en masse, and foreign investment drying up. Observers are also beginning to appreciate the negative environmental impact of Dubai-style development. Such an about-face is a result of Dubai's particularly volatile location in the global economy. It also shows what a moving target Dubai is and how difficult it is to write something about the city more durable than much of the journalism produced over the last few years.[2]

The collapse of the neoliberal press's regard for the city is a reflection of the collapse of a global economy—and a global urban landscape—largely shaped by the volatile principles of neoliberalism: financial deregulation, increasing dependence on foreign investment, and an overreliance on an "artistic mode of (urban) production,"[3] among other factors. Therefore, what were until the crash grounds for celebration of Dubai as an avant-garde experiment in globalization—the so-called diversification of the economy away from oil extraction and export toward sectors such as foreign investment, tourism, real estate, and the construction of gargantuan landscapes of "bourgeois gratification"[4]—have, for the time being, become examples of Dubai's deep flaws. The glitzy experiment without (we were told) limits to its growth has now become an economic crater, too reliant on the very sectors of the economy most vulnerable to the kind of downturn the world is experiencing.

Obviously, at least one of these theories cannot be true. But does it follow that the other must be correct by default? Or is the truth somewhere in between? This book attempts to approach Dubai in a more sober way than has been characteristic of much if not most coverage of the city since its rise to global prominence in the mid-1990s. Sobriety, in discussing Dubai, is in itself an achievement. There have been few if any other cities in the Middle East that have elicited as much hype. One writer, in an important American cultural magazine, asserted that Dubai was gripped by an "architectural insanity";[5] another writer averred, rather, that the city is a diamond of progress in the notional Arab forest of backwardness.[6] The hype, however, is not without basis. Enormous buildings and landscape projects shaped like palm trees and maps of the world will tend to attract attention, and this is far from unintentional. Yet the questions of why the rulers and various elites, such as large landlords, saw such development as rational and how Dubai's development path is influenced by both its social and political structures and the everyday practices of its urbanists are ones that this sensationalizing journalism seems particularly badly situated to answer. The aim of this book is two-fold: to provide both socio-historical and theoretical context to emancipate Dubai, or more accurately "Dubai," from journalistic cant; and to theorize—modestly, provisionally, and self-critically—possible lessons for twenty-first-century urbanism, especially in the arena of the so-called global south.

Along with its UAE neighbors Abu Dhabi and Ras al-Khayma, Dubai during the first decade of the twenty-first century recruited a stable of star architects such as Frank Gehry, Zaha Hadid, and Rem Koolhaas to design attention-grabbing projects. Although most of this book was written and compiled before Dubai's "starchitect" phase, this example of the city's vast program of urban entrepreneurialism confirms the insights brought forth in the following chapters. In Dubai, as Kevin Mitchell puts it, the emphasis is on the building itself, especially the aesthetic form, and not on urban design or sound planning. Further, as I argue in my contribution, both local elites and foreign boosters of the city see Dubai's urban space as a commodity.[7] Recent urban scholarship has begun to point to the intensifying competition between cities for a higher profile in the global economy of images. Dubai's seemingly interminable search for superlatives (the tallest skyscraper, the world's first underwater hotel, the world's only seven-star resort, etc.) is part of this broader phenomenon. Hence the title of this volume.

In his seminal recent work, *Urban Theory: A Critical Assessment,* John Rennie Short summarizes the global urban situation since the late twentieth century. With the shift of industrial production from the industrialized to the developing world and the bifurcation of command and productive functions, unprecedented numbers of cities across the globe compete to be both command centers and places of "world spectacle."[8] The result is a legion of "wannabe" global cities, such as Taipei, Kuala Lumpur, Beijing, and of course Dubai:

Wannabe world cities particularly concern themselves with ensuring the most effective international image possible by having all the attributes of a global city. Such prerequisites include an international airport, signature buildings of big name architects ... and cultural complexes such as art spaces and symphony halls.[9]

Wannabe cities are "cities of spectacle ... and powerful growth rhetoric."[10] It is thus no accident that Dubai has almost all of the characteristics outlined by Short. The appearance of the high-profile architects, with their impressive projects—museums (Tadao Ando, Gehry, Hadid, Jean Nouvel), opera houses (Hadid), conference centers (Snøhetta), and planned "sustainable" cities-within-cities (Norman Foster, Koolhaas)—is the logical next step in Dubai's and Abu Dhabi's attempts to compete in a crowded global city market. In this connection, as Neyran Turan points out in this volume, Dubai is an offspring of Bilbao. Both Turan's and Stephen Ramos and Peter Rowe's chapters highlight the prototypical and modular character of Dubai urbanism. Not only does this approach, as Ramos and Rowe argue, enable efficient responses to rapid demographic and urban-morphological changes, it also (according to Turan) makes Dubai urbanism highly exportable and applicable in diverse global contexts.

The aforementioned journalism on Dubai misses much of this, evincing a breathless fascination with what is tiresomely called the "iconic" architecture of the city. Much that appears to be perplexing about Dubai from the aesthetic or architectural level ("Palm Islands! How do they do it?!"), begins after the interventions made in this volume to make sense, and to appear a little less exotic, a little less the concoction of the overheated imagination of an Albert Speer on "the shores of Araby."[11] As Ramos and Rowe argue in "Planning, Prototyping, and Replication in Dubai," the infrastructure and principles from which development proceeds are necessarily flexible, strategically dispensing with an intricate master plan. One significant example they cite is land reclamation, which uses the stream of dredge spoils from nearby in a rational way, keeping sea lanes open. In one important respect, this flexibility is historical. The focus on the locational scale, as opposed to that of the urban, developed about ten years before the independence in 1971 of the United Arab Emirates, when the Dubai state (Dubai is an "emirate," in English, imprecisely, a "principality," of the UAE) began taking over lands not registered to landowners. The state acted, in other words, as one among several landlords, primus inter pares, to be sure, but operating with a general respect for the interests of the landlord. These land plots were therefore developed with mercantile intentions, each landlord seeking to maximize his or her profits. For Ramos and Rowe, the underlying logic of this is eminently rational. There is a reappraisal here of modernist orthodoxy, which tended to see landlord capitalism as resulting inevitably in chaos. The logic of Dubai's approach, for Ramos and Rowe, is evidenced by the fact that not chaos, but an alertness and sensitivity to exogenous demands and an openness to future uncertainties result from prototyping, amplification, and replication.

This recuperation of the rational is a welcome corrective to the reductive picture of the city as merely a copy of Western modernity. This is the theme of Amale Andraos and Dan Wood's chapter, "Peak Urbanism, Micro-Planning, and Other Emergent

Realities in Dubai." What Ramos and Rowe term "the locational," Andraos and Wood theorize as the "micro-plan." For Andraos and Wood, this is also evidence of Dubai's flexibility, a skill developed to deal with the rapidity of urbanization since the 1970s. But there is a pitfall here, as what is seen from one angle as a tactical response to macro conditions of windfall wealth and the management of a demographic boom becomes, from another angle, an invitation to developers to create redundant themed enclaves at the expense of both necessary infrastructures and sound urban design and planning. Nevertheless, Andraos and Wood counsel patience, as Dubai is still in many ways an urban work-in-progress: like Ramos and Rowe, they see in "micro-plans" a potential openness to changing urban and geographical conditions that resist totalitarian implications.

For Boris Brorman Jensen, this flexibility might become symptomatic of urbanism in the early twenty-first century. Drawing on geographers Michael Dear and Steven Flusty, Jensen argues in his chapter "Learning from Dubai" that Dubai's is a landscape of "keno capitalism." Here a highly abstract grid or pattern is mapped onto space: the gaming-board-like zoning practice whereby the municipality vaguely plans the primary functions of the infrastructural system. This leaves the game wide open, such that (in Jensen's vivid analogy) "the incoherent pattern of private development projects descends from above like pieces that have been drawn in some external investment game with no relations of physical proximity." Although Jensen makes a strong case that this urban type may become the successor of the concentric city of the early twentieth century, there is, as I point out in my chapter, "Dubai, in Particular," one important archaism that has not been overcome. The metaphor of the bingo board, with the private enclaves as gaming pieces "descending" from on high, assumes a specific perspective: that of the airplane or "God's-eye" view. Here we are on familiar territory: as I try to show in my reading of Dubai ruler Sheikh Muhammad bin Rashid Al Maktum as a restyled baroque prince, the "God-planner" is the stock-in-trade of high modernism, from its origins in the European renaissance through the mid-twentieth century.[12]

Jensen makes another stimulating point, this one echoed by Gareth Doherty and Virginie Picon-Lefebvre in their respective analyses of landscape. In the absence of a recent master plan (Dubai's second and last was conceived by John Harris of the British engineering firm Halcrow in 1971, as Ramos and Rowe discuss in their chapter), unconventional elements have been inadvertently pressed into the service of a quasi plan: golf, according to Jensen, has become the universal master plan, with the Dubai Creekside Golf club providing the prototype for more recent gated communities such as Nakheel's The Gardens and EMAAR's Emirates Hills. For Doherty, it is not simply greens that qualify as "landscape." This view, he argues, has tended to represent both landscape and architecture as inert, lacking in agency. Rather, the whole city should be seen as a (living, fluid) landscape. For Doherty, architecture tends too often to treat building and landscape as separate domains, with the latter taking a subordinate role. Dubai, for Doherty, shows how building and landscape complexly interact. The building sets off a sort of rhizomal reaction triggering shifts in the landscape, as the case of the Dubai World Trade Center of the late 1970s demonstrates. Conventional understandings, as applied in Dubai, however, valorize images of green landscapes. This is misguided, he believes, leading to an approach that is energy- and water-intensive. Doherty argues for a more layered and complex understanding of landscape, which sees it as an integral part of the thick fabric of urbanism, not merely as residual to building and urban planning. Thus Doherty seems more skeptical of notions such as "prototyping and replication" (Ramos and Rowe) and the "micro-plan" (Andraos and Wood), seeing less thought, reason, or "planning" in such phenomena (this is a theme that will be picked up, in the latter half of the volume, by Mitchell's more empirical analysis of the flaws of Dubai architecture).

In her chapter, "Dubai Manifesto," Virginie Picon-Lefebvre sees Dubai not as an updated modernist "green city" but rather as a postindustrial "blue city." Contrary to what is popularly assumed, she argues, not everything is gated in Dubai. The shore of the Creek *(Khor Dubai)* and other waterscapes seem to her to offer the possibility of a real publicness. This Dubai is seen as a complex but essentially water-focused city, one of the latest in a long line of resort and spa towns that draw their model from Europe. European resorts and spas developed in the late eighteenth and nineteenth centuries, when the urban–water interface no longer signified fear and filth, but rather health and leisure. While developing this point, Picon-Lefebvre also explains one of the puzzling aspects of design in Dubai: the prevalence of so much theming. The tendency among critics has been to dismiss theming as simply "bad taste." Yet according to her, the penchant for eclecticism is characteristic also of nineteenth-century European spas and seaside resorts. Although now familiar from landscapes of cultural consumption and entertainment such as theme parks, Dubai's application of theming seems unique because of its larger, urban scale.

The second argument that Picon-Lefebvre makes is taken up by both Neyran Turan ("The Dubai Effect Archipelago") and Yasser Elsheshtawy ("Situating the Dubai Spectacle"). Picon-Lefebvre sees great potential in geographies of water to trouble the hegemony of privatized space in Dubai. In the many beach parks and dense, human-scaled, and walkable area of the Khor, she sees something almost typical of traditions of pluralistic urbanity of the Middle East and Indian Ocean: for her, the water of Dubai "generates a new lifestyle," inviting people from different social and national backgrounds to mix in spaces without visible boundaries. From Picon-Lefebvre's essay, the reader senses that the developers of newer, more dazzling projects such as the Palm Islands would do well to learn from these understated spaces.[13] Echoing Doherty, however, she ends the chapter on a less sanguine note. She warns that Dubai has thus far too unquestioningly drawn on landscape and architectural legacies developed in Europe, such as, again, green landscapes, which are too water-intensive and unsustainable.

Turan is also interested in the new lifestyles and models proposed by Dubai, but she addresses a global rather than an urban scale. Focusing on one company, EMAAR, Turan's chapter is an arresting glimpse into what could be in store. Founded in the late 1990s by Sheikh Muhammad, EMAAR is one of several important developers of skyscrapers, gated communities, and themed resorts under the umbrella of the Sheikh's business empire (Nakheel and Dubai Properties being two others).[14] Turan's illuminating discussion shows how EMAAR is both a typically Imarati company—a product of the specific history of Dubai—and an exportable model from a region, the Gulf, more accustomed to exporting raw materials than intellectual products or concepts.

EMAAR is a good case study in Dubai's post-independence trajectory and the increasing centralization and authoritarianism of the Maktum regime. EMAAR, Nakheel, and other Maktum firms are usually seen as examples of the foresight of the Dubai rulers. They are, the theory goes, part of a broader agenda of modernization. Moreover, they seem to demonstrate the regime's progressive and "visionary" character. This assumption flows from the scholarship on the UAE, which has tended to represent the ascent of the ruling dynasties in Abu Dhabi, Dubai, and other emirates as both inevitable and a triumph of stability.

There are significant problems with this theory. Most important, there is nothing inevitable about the rise of the Maktum. To assume that a ruling regime's rise was inevitable is to implicitly agree with its version of history. Recently, a critique of the Maktum-centered narrative has been launched from the left. As Mike Davis has correctly suggested, EMAAR owes its success to the neoliberal practice of the privatization of the state, implying that Dubai's "success" is really a combination of authoritarianism and capital-friendly policies.[15] The Maktum firms of EMAAR, Nakheel, and Dubai Holding, for example, are private companies chaired, respectively, by Muhammad al-Abbar, Ali Rashid, Ahmad Lootah, and Muhammad al-Gergawi. Simultaneously, these companies have public or state façades and functions (such as some financial operations, and, in effect, an urban planning mandate from Sheikh Muhammad). Thus al-Abbar, Lootah, and al-Gergawi become government ministers as well.

But while Davis's critique is useful in pointing the out the points of ideological alignment between the global neoliberal order and local social formations that enact neoliberal policies, it does not say much about the role of local and regional historical factors in the rise of the Maktum and its current spatial politics. EMAAR, Nakheel, and other Maktum companies account for the bulk of urban and real estate development in the emirate. This means, in effect, that the Maktum regime has overwhelming power to decide what kinds of buildings are built and what kind of policy agenda is to be furthered by construction. As Doherty has shown, infrastructures and "landscape" often follow building and are reactions to it. The predominance of EMAAR et al. in urban development means that the form of the city, and by extension its political-economic order, ultimately flows from the dictates of Maktum. Will the city be a place of vibrant, participatory public spaces or a fragmentary landscape of privatized enclaves? What say will local people have over tourism policy or guidelines on respecting local customs? How are local people to be integrated into the private sector? What about more complicated issues such as who decides the meaning of the term "national wealth," whether this is substantively different from existing structures of paternalist distribution, and what is to be the ideal relationship between locals and immigrants? Dubai's contemporary (urban, political, and social) landscape has taken shape largely through Maktum dictating the city's responses to these questions and marginalizing other voices. After coopting or crushing reformist and nationalist movements at various points in the first half the twentieth century, the Rashid bin Said branch of the Maktum consolidated their monopoly over the emirate. Two main factors accelerated this process: first, British intervention, both in the elevation of the Rashid bin Said branch in Dubai before UAE independence and in giving the post-independence UAE its shape as a federated, dynastic, authoritarian state; and second, the oil boom of the 1970s.

Throughout the Indian Ocean, the British invented dynasts and provided them with mythically deep histories and sovereignty over the societies that were to be absorbed into the Empire. Like their erstwhile counterparts in the Malay Straits and British India, the dynasts of the Gulf were elevated to the role of centralizing autocrats over their societies. Like in Malaya and India, there was (contrary to Maktum-centered histories that are hegemonic today) resistance to the British-imposed regime. But resistance was crushed, either by Maktum violence or other means.[16] Reflecting on the demise of one reformist upsurge in the first half of the twentieth century, a prominent Dubai merchant put it this way: the British feared "what they saw as the emergence of progressive tendencies ... and the establishment of (popular bodies) actually representative of the community."[17] "It would be easier," he adds, "to keep dealing with the traditional tribal structures than the more diffuse, less predictable activities of popular assemblies."[18]

Unlike in the Malay Straits or India, however, the British-imposed regimes in the Gulf were not succeeded by robust, independent nationalist states. These regimes remained in place and, with oil income sweeping away the last vestiges of nationalist and reformist resistance, they became more powerful and centralized. In short, a regime, the Maktum, which was historically more attuned to imperial rather than popular interests, transitioned in the post-independence period into a more powerful version of its colonial identity. In its contemporary form it carries out three main functions: the management of its oil monopoly and land near-monopoly, the distribution and protection of exclusive commercial rights for an elite from among the national population, and the mutually advantageous handling of an elite, primarily Western-based stratum of experts, managers, and technocrats from among the expatriate population.[19]

As Waleed Hazbun writes in an analysis of the politics of tourism in the Arab world, within the Maktum-controlled land regime, "the ruler may sell the land, lease it, put it to special uses over a set period, or allocate it to the municipality for public utilities ... Even those with property rights have only limited autonomy over the range of uses they may make of it."[20] Hazbun calls this a regime of "total territorial control," and among its other functions is the creation of dependent social classes by providing housing for citizens and managing private-sector development, part of a deal in which the state "is never required to grant any means for political participation or popular accountability."[21] Within this regime of "total territorial control," institutions such as EMAAR and Nakheel are permitted to develop specific kinds of urban space—tourist and shopping-oriented landscapes of "bourgeois gratification" (as Diane Ghirardo has put it) and private enclaves for well-to-do global expatriates—without any popular participation or criticism.[22]

During the period of my most intensive fieldwork between 2003 and 2006, I routinely spoke to expatriates from the developing world, such as Arabs and Indians, who admitted (albeit sometimes reluctantly) how impressed they were with what Dubai was doing, especially when they compared the (at that time) efficient infrastructures and seeming market-consumer prosperity of the Emirati city to their experiences in Bombay, Cairo, etc. Although one wonders whether these expatriates are so sanguine about Dubai today (and whether any of them are among those fleeing Dubai), there is something deeper to these comments than simple neoliberal ideology. This is the significance of Turan's chapter. Dubai, she shows, has converted its local model of landlord-capitalism into an idiom that is inherently cosmopolitan and global: that of modern, capital-friendly architecture and urbanism. Elsheshtawy's chapter describes a similar process in Egypt. The IT parastatal of the former ruling Mubarak regime, modeled on Dubai's Media City and Knowledge Village, and shopping mall and shopping festival projects by the Dubai tycoon Majid Al Futtaim are exemplary of what Elsheshtawy calls the "Dubaization" of many cities in the Arab region. Although it did not initially catch on, a major Futtaim mall project has become successful in recent years. While franchises such as the seemingly inevitable Starbucks cater to a wealthier clientele, the Carrefour hypermarket, offering low-cost goods, has become popular with classes of more modest means. For the time being, the Futtaim malls stands alone, with land surrounding it undeveloped.[23]

The next chapters shift the focus to historical, social, and local conditions. In my chapter, "Dubai, in Particular." I look at what I call "the anomalous spaces and ignored histories" for which there are no neat expressions (verbal, imagistic, or otherwise) in the spatial and urbanistic languages of neoliberalism. Adapting a distinction from Henri Lefebvre between "abstract space" and "differential space," I show how the former, in the particular guise of Maktum projects such as the Palm Jebel Ali, are not simply whimsical, postmodernist, politically innocent spaces. There is a stylistic resonance between such spaces and those of the high modernist tradition: sculptural, enormous, and functionally monochromatic. These are spaces of power, both projecting and revealing a particular spatial "vision" (to adapt a phrase from James Scott), that of the absolutist, centralized dynastic state. That a purely formal architectural fascination with Dubai ignores this is revealing, both of the dynastic state's success in aligning its vision of power and space with that of the global media, and of a strong tendency in the global architectural profession to consider irrelevant or secondary any but the formal aspects of building. My survey of some everyday modes by which Dubayyans invest their urban experience with meaning is meant to bring other voices into the conversation, highlighting the less elite, more locally situated interpretations of Dubai's recent trajectory.

The story is further complicated by the account of Maryam Monalisa Gharavi, who presents one of the troubling aspects of the contemporary scene in Dubai: the struggles of so-called guest workers, immigrants who work in services, construction, and other labor-intensive, low-wage sectors that have expanded with the post-1970s boom economy. Focusing on construction workers, Gharavi adds a theoretical and critical dimension to Ramos and Rowe's image of a state-elite complex that, at a planning level, is flexible and more or less rational.

Gharavi's contribution suggests that the study of Dubai can inform broader issues, such as analysis of the connections between politics, power, culture, and globalization.[24] How is the global order produced, not only as a result of reconfigurations of the capitalist economy away from manufacturing and toward services and financial operations, but also as a political project of various formations of privilege, as well as geographies and gradients of inequality, within the capitalist economy? How, following David Harvey, do space and geography function to produce and reproduce capital accumulation and inequality?[25] And what is the relation of local structures of meaning and local practices of capitalism to the reproduction of global power relations?

A second issue where Gharavi's chapter is suggestive is the relationship between empirical cases and models. Urbanists have focused disproportionate attention on the metropolitan centers of the North/West in comparison to cities in the developing world or "global south." Our notion of the development of the city in the modern period seems inevitably to refer to the experiences of a few usual suspects: New York, Los Angeles, Paris, and Tokyo.[26]

If situated alongside other cases from the global south, Dubai can reveal new insights about how cities develop outside North America and Western Europe. Conventional notions of the Western industrial/postindustrial city frame this urban type within an economic historiography that assumes the existence of bounded nation-states with industrial economies and major cities assuming command and production roles in processes of state formation. Scholars focusing on the state, space, and globalization within non-Western contexts, however, have found urban space to be more fragmented and diffuse, arguably more characterized by a "graduated sovereignty" (as Aihwa Ong has put it), than a focus on the global north would suggest.[27] Dubai, for example, is a platform for the mobility of humans, capital, and commodities from a large surrounding region marked by political volatility and neoliberal-induced disorder. Its functional, economic, and cultural connections to surrounding nation-states have developed diversely: it is a financial center (UAE, Iran, South Asia), a labor importer (South Asia, Iran, the Arab countries, the former USSR), an exporter of cultural capital (Africa, Europe, Middle East, South Asia), a reexport platform (Europe, North America, South Asia, and many others), a military and naval port (United States), and a refinance center, especially within the real estate sector (Iran, former USSR, and various others).

While Gharavi targets Dubai's political-economic context, Kevin Mitchell's equally strong critique aims at the city's architecture and design. What seems to make sense from the landscape or quasi-planning perspective is, from another viewpoint—that of urban design—chaotic, the result of a "myopic focus on individual buildings at the expense of cohesive urban plans." Here we might have reached the limits of the flexible, locationally focused model that had guided Dubai through an eventful twentieth century of economic and demographic crises and booms. In the early twenty-first century, Dubai's aspirations in the financial and symbolic economies of the global order might have finally outpaced this model (something discussed at length by Andraos and Wood). Mitchell describes a troubling situation in which speed of construction is privileged over quality of construction and easily consumable, unsustainable, decorative architecture over anything of lasting quality; architecture becomes, in Hannah Arendt's terms, an object of consumption rather than one of culture. But Mitchell's critique is not purely aesthetic. If meeting the human needs for "beauty," "commodity" (i.e., social interaction), and "durability," as well as cultivating reciprocity between the built environment and the natural environment, continue to be the aims of architecture, then Dubai architecture repeatedly fails.[28]

This book goes to press at a moment of profound change in the Arab world. History is full of ironies. When we the contributors to this volume began conceptualizing the project of this book, Dubai and Dubai-like projects around the Arab region seemed to many of us to be where the urban and political future of the region—and perhaps other regions as well—was heading. Now we are not so sure. After their astonishing revolutions of late 2010–2011, Egypt and Tunisia look forward to a future beyond the model of the security state dominated by one family, which has blighted the region for so long. Libyans, Yemenis, and especially Syrians have also taken on entrenched one-family states, but at far higher cost and with much more future uncertainly. In the Gulf, the status quo was momentarily shaken, with protests in Bahrain triggering a rescue of the ruling Al Khalifa by the Saudi Arabian military. It is impossible at this juncture to predict where the region will go. The UAE and a few other exceptions seem to be unaffected by the events of the Arab spring, a testament to the iron grip of the ruling dynasties of these emirates. Sadat's separate peace with Begin in the late 1970s marginalized Egypt from its leading role in shaping Arab politics and culture. The civil war of 1975–1991 did something similar to Lebanon. In this vacuum, powered by petrodollars and relative stability, the states of the Gulf began to take the leadership role in matters political, cultural, and urban in the Arab region. This situation created an opening for Dubai, which for a time became the model of Arab urbanism. Perhaps now the Arab Spring will restore some of the older leaders, not least Egypt and Cairo, as they carve out a path more independent of U.S. empire and perhaps of neoliberalism. The book goes to press during exciting, uncertain times, times that raise more questions than easy answers and invite an attitude of questioning and reflection.

Taken collectively, the essays in this volume—although sometimes reaching different conclusions about and drawing different lessons from Dubai—are united in their questioning, critical spirit. Rather than provide answers, the contributors prefer to continue probing. How do emerging cities and urban regions in the contemporary world trouble our political and theoretical assumptions about, for example, the bounded nation-state and the relationships between urbanism and capitalism? How are rapid economic and urban changes used by cities to advantageously situate themselves at the borderlands of the global economy? How do the diverse interconnections between different cities and urban regions relate to issues of territorial sovereignty? How are urban and spatial images and technologies that emerge in specific times and places transposed to other, very different contexts? These are a few of the questions raised by the chapters in this volume, showing that the case of Dubai is worthy of far more serious attention that it has received so far and that it constitutes a rich vein for future research.

Notes

I wish to thank the students of my seminar, "The Making of Modern Dubai," which I taught at Trinity College in Spring 2009, for discussions and papers that advanced my thinking on Dubai's trajectory. I am especially grateful to Emily Forsyth and Mollie Landry, from whose research into the issues of Dubai's impact on the ecology and the effects of the economic crisis on Dubai, respectively, I have learned a great deal.

1   Matthew Brown, "Hadid Leading Architectural Rush to the Emirates," *International Herald Tribune*, April 3, 2008.

2   For scholarly sources on Dubai, see contributor Stephen Ramos's *Dubai Amplified: The Engineering of a Port Geography* (Farnham, Surrey, UK: Ashgate, 2010); Christopher M. Davidson, *Dubai: The Vulnerability of Success* (New York: Columbia University Press, 2008); Waleed Hazbun, *Beaches, Ruins, Resorts: The Politics of Tourism in the Arab World* (Minneapolis: University of Minnesota Press, 2008); Ahmed Kanna, *Dubai, The City as Corporation* (Minneapolis: University of Minnesota Press, 2011); and Neha Vora, *Impossible Citizens: Dubai's Indian Diaspora* (Durham, NC: Duke University Press, 2013). In many ways, one of the best works on the UAE remains Abdul-Khaleq Abdulla's 1984 PhD dissertation, *Political Dependency: The Case of the United Arab Emirates*, Department of Government, Georgetown University. While much of its technical language is dated, it is one of the more frank and theoretically informed analyses of political economy in the UAE and Dubai. Thanks to Arang Keshavarzian for referring me to this document.

3   Sharon Zukin, *Loft Living: Culture and Capital in Urban Change* (New Brunswick NJ: Rutgers University Press), p. 176.

4   Diane Ghirardo, *Out of Site: A Social Criticism of Architecture* (Seattle: Bay Press, 1991), p. 15.

5   Ian Parker, "The Mirage: The Architectural Insanity of Dubai," *New Yorker*, October 17, 2005, pp. 128–143.

6   Thomas Friedman, "Dubai and Dunces," *New York Times*, March 15, 2006.

7   I describe the rise of celebrity architecture and some prominent projects in the UAE, such as Hadid's Dubai Opera House, Koolhaas's Dubai Waterfront City, and the respective Abu Dhabi projects by Ando, Gehry, and Foster, in chapter 2 of *Dubai, The City as Corporation*.

8   John Rennie Short, *Urban Theory: A Critical Assessment* (New York: Palgrave Macmillan, 2006), p. 113.

9   Ibid., p. 114.

10 Ibid., p. 115.

11 As Mike Davis puts it in "Dubai: Sinister Paradise," *Mother Jones*, July 14, 2005. http://www.motherjones.com/commentary/columns/2005/07/sinister_paradise.html

12 Here I am drawing on James C. Scott, *Seeing Like a State: How Certain Schemes to Improve the Human Condition Have Failed* (New Haven: Yale University Press, 1998).

13 The distinction that Lefebvre makes between such spaces is one of general significance and is by now standard in architecture and planning criticism. It transcribes the categorical distinction between what are sometimes referred to as "spaces of power" and "popular spaces" and is common as

well in ethnography, sociology, and the analysis of the politics of space. See, for example, Khaled Adham, "Globalization, Neoliberalism, and New Spaces of Capital in Cairo," *Traditional Dwellings and Settlements Review* 17, 1 (Fall 2005), and Peter Marcuse, "Tradition in a Global City?," *Traditional Dwellings and Settlements Review* 17, 2 (Spring 2006). In this book, the distinction reappears, for example, in my own discussion (chapter 9) of what I call "the Old Dubai," centered on the urban core of the pre-1970s boom, the Khor (Creek), and the "New Dubai," the corridor that has since the 1990s been the locus of neoliberal enclave and subdivision development under the aegis of Sheikh Muhammad's firms and those of various large landlords (e.g., Majid Al Futtaim).

14 See www.emaar.com, www.nakheel.com, and www.dubai-properties.ae. Sheikh Muhammad is not the only serious player. Other major landlords, such as Majid Al Futtaim and Saif Al Ghurair, exercise immense local, and increasing global, power. See, for example, Elsheshtawy's "Situating the Dubai Spectacle," this volume, on Al Futtaim's City Centre concept as a means for exporting the "Dubai Model."

15 Mike Davis, "Fear and Money in Dubai," *New Left Review* 41 (September–October 2006), especially pp. 60–64.

16 Davidson, *Dubai*, pp. 34–35.

17 Ibid., p. 35.

18 Ibid.

19 Abdulla, *Political Dependency: The Case of the United Arab Emirates*, pp. 123–124.

20 Hazbun, *Beaches, Ruins, Resorts*, p. 217.

21 Ibid.

22 Ghirardo, *Out of Site*, p. 15.

23 Elsheshtawy adds that while the center was substantially damaged by looters during the early days of the 2011 Egyptian Revolution, it was re-opened shortly after the revolution, with the Dubai developer Al Futtaim announcing plans on continuing Dubai-style projects in Egypt, including a Cairo Festival City located nearby. Yasser Elsheshtawy, personal communication, June 19, 2011.

24 See, for example, Arjun Appadurai, *Modernity at Large: Cultural Dimensions of Globalization* (Minneapolis: University of Minnesota Press, 1996); James Ferguson, *Global Shadows: Africa in the Neoliberal World Order* (Durham: Duke University Press, 2006); Aihwa Ong, *Neoliberalism as Exception: Mutations of Citizenship and Sovereignty* (Durham: Duke University Press, 2007); James L. Watson, ed., *Golden Arches East: McDonald's in East Asia* (Palo Alto: Stanford University Press, 1997).

25 David Harvey, "Reinventing Geography," *New Left Review* 4 (July/August 2000).

26 For an extended discussion and critique of this tendency, see Xiangming Chen and Ahmed Kanna, eds., *Rethinking Global Urbanism: Comparative Insights from Secondary Cities* (New York: Routledge, 2012).

27 Port cities are an exception in the developed world: as transshipment hubs, cities such as Dubai and Shenzhen have many similarities with ports in the developed world such as Rotterdam, Los Angeles, etc. For examples of

work on the state, space, and neoliberalism in non-Western contexts, see James Ferguson, *Global Shadows* and "Seeing Like an Oil Company: Space, Security, and Global Capital in Neoliberal Africa," *American Anthropologist* 107, 3 (2005), pp. 377–382; James Ferguson and Akhil Gupta, "Spatializing States: Toward an Ethnography of Neoliberal Governmentality," *American Ethnologist* 29, 4 (2002), pp. 981–1002; Tania Murray Li, "Beyond 'the State' and Failed Schemes," *American Anthropologist* 107, 3 (2005), pp. 383–394; Roland Marchal, "Dubai: Global City and Transnational Hub," in Madawi al-Rasheed, ed., *Transnational Connections and the Arab Gulf* (New York: Routledge, 2005), pp. 93–110; Aihwa Ong, "Graduated Sovereignty in South-East Asia," *Theory,* *Culture & Society* 17, 4 (2000), pp. 55–75 ; Smriti Srinivas, *Landscapes of Urban Memory: The Sacred and the Civic in India's High-Tech City* (Minneapolis: University of Minnesota Press, 2001); Anna Lowenhaupt Tsing, *Friction: An Ethnography of Global Connection* (Princeton: Princeton University Press, 2005); Ara Wilson, *The Intimate Economies of Bangkok: Tomboys, Tycoons, and Avon Ladies in the Global City* (Berkeley: University of California Press, 2004).

28   For a discussion of "commodity, beauty, and durability," see Witold Rybczinski's essay, *The Look of Architecture* (New York: Oxford University Press, 2001).

STEPHEN RAMOS
AND PETER G. ROWE

2

PLANNING, PROTOTYPING, AND REPLICATION IN DUBAI

Dubai grew dramatically over the past fifty years, moving beyond its original walled settlement around the mouth of its creek to become an aspiring global city. Within this time, Dubai transformed from a modest trading post, refueling stop for commercial aircraft, and territorial concession for oil exploration on the Arabian Gulf into a diversified and rapidly growing city. The population, which was barely 250,000 people in the late 1970s, has since more than quadrupled.[1] In the face of this urban expansion, conventional planning, which first appeared on the scene during the late 1950s, gave way to a predominance of interrelated large-scale developments, most of which were responsive to a matrix of global flows of goods, services, and capital. Spatially and logistically organized around almost equally rapidly evolving armatures of infrastructure, development sites spread out across a broad area of otherwise desert terrain running parallel to the coast, stretching some 50 kilometers, from Sharjah west toward Abu Dhabi. Far from conforming to an overall master plan, each specific swath of development has its own internal logic and environmental character, the sum of which appear as a yet-to-be-completed mosaic. Consciously or not, over the past twenty years or more, once a successful form for a particular type of development arose, it became a prototype for subsequent developments of a similar kind. Often, during this process of replication, aspects of the prototype were also amplified, usually to meet higher demands. Thus Port Rashid gave rise to the massive Jebel Ali Port, the Dubai World Trade Center to Burj Dubai, the Dubai International Airport to the Al Maktoum International Airport, the Palm Jumeirah to the World, and so on, across different kinds of development. Furthermore, this process of prototyping, amplification, and replication, once specific locational requirements were satisfied, allowed Dubai to closely mirror exogenous demands, remain open to future uncertainties, and develop more or less at will, without the potential strictures of a predetermined master plan. To the extent that it is practiced, planning was confined to broad locational decisions about developments, to the developments themselves, and to major elements of infrastructure such as roads, canals, ports, and airports, as well as to utility and service improvements. This, however, was not always the case and may need to change if and when the mosaic pattern, referred to earlier, nears completion.

EARLY SETTLEMENT

Dubai began as a port. The *Khor Dubai,* or Dubai Creek, in spite of the silt building up at its mouth, offered appropriate environmental conditions in an otherwise hostile coast, which helped Dubai become one of the principal ports of the Gulf region from the seventeenth century. European powers, beginning with the Venetians and then with the Portuguese, the Dutch, and finally the British, were interested in the Gulf region as a means to secure trade routes (silk and spice, among others) to and from the Indian subcontinent and points eastward. This meant that from the fifteenth century through the late nineteenth century, if trade routes could move uninterrupted through the Gulf region, European powers were not involved in the societal affairs of settlements as a traditional colonial ruling class, nor did European merchants bother to extensively explore trade within the region, believing that it required more effort than either the climate or the local economies were worth.[2] Local tribes of the region were divided among the maritime coastal groups and those that were nomadic and land-bound, and throughout the nineteenth century, the rivaling tribes of the Qawasim (of Persian origin) and the Bani Yas (from the Najd region) competed for trade and territorial influence between their respective ports of Sharjah and Abu Dhabi. In 1833, 800 members of the Al Bu Falasa subsection of the Al Maktoum family left Abu Dhabi to settle in a point between Sharjah and Abu Dhabi, and this is understood as the birth of modern Dubai.

Since the late eighteenth century, British trade routes were often disturbed by pirate attacks on their ships in the southern Gulf region, which prompted a series of expeditions of the British government to the region to broker agreements with the various coastal tribes. In 1820, the General Treaty of Peace was signed, followed by the Ten-Year Maritime Truce in 1843, and finally the Perpetual Treaty of Truce in 1853, which called for an end to piracy along the trade routes and stipulated for the British government to "watch over and protect" the southern Gulf region "for evermore."[3] The treaty also baptized the region under the new name of Trucial Oman, or the Trucial States.

Just how long pearl fishing was practiced along the coasts of Dubai is a topic of great speculation, but what is clear is that by the late nineteenth century it was the principal economic activity of the region. Other than fish, which provided the city its main staple, there were no other natural resources to support the economy, and pearl fishing and trade grew rapidly. Merchants from Persia and India were attracted to the Trucial Coast by pearl-fishing opportunities, and this group would steadily grow into an important merchant class that had a strong voice in the governing and investment decisions

Page 18: High-rise construction along Sheikh Zayed Road
Aerial Photo of Dubai in 1976, with Port Rashid visible at the mouth of the Khor Dubai Creek

1976

Aerial Photo of the Maktoum Bridge in the early 1960s

of Dubai.[4] In the later part of the nineteenth century, the Dubai coast harvested a good portion of the pearls for the international market, and the port's early settlers, along with the ruling family, were principally those who worked in the pearl-harvesting sector.

With an increasing integration into British trade routes, Dubai's role as an international port became more significant. In the late 1870s, for instance, Britain declared Dubai its principal port of the Trucial States for British merchants. By 1890 the Bombay and Persia Steam Navigation Company had moved from Sharjah to Dubai and, by 1905, some thirty-four steamers were calling regularly, raising the annual volume of cargo to 70,000 tons.[5] About the same time, Tehran imposed restrictive Imperial Customs tariffs and controls on all goods for reexport in the Bandar Lingeh port, at the time the major port of the Gulf, to Dubai. In what would prove to be a regional coup, in 1904 the ruler of Dubai, Maktoum bin Hashar, at the *majlis* (council of the merchant class), declared the Dubai port to be tax-free and control-free, and this quickly attracted reexport activities from Bandar Lingeh across the Gulf to the Dubai port.[6] All commerce between Great Britain and India would then pass through Dubai, firmly establishing Dubai's vocation as a strategic entrepôt for British imperial trade routes. As a result, the merchant class greatly benefited from the rapid increase in trade throughput.

Dubai grew steadily through the early part of the twentieth century, and World War I had little effect on its prosperous trading activity. It was the Japanese who would deal the first blow to the Dubai economy with the introduction of the cultured pearl. This, along with the world recession of 1929, had a great impact on Dubai's economy, and a new form of resource trade was needed to replace the pearls that had helped to support the small but growing urban population. Then, beginning in the 1930s, Dubai was able to leverage its geographic importance by selling oil exploration concessions and developing an aviation infrastructure. The Creek's linear form helped make the port attractive for inland trading and access, but in the 1930s, its form also inspired the British to establish a floating airbase. The British Imperial Airways set up the airstrip in 1937, and Dubai's physical characteristics were used to advantage to further its role as an important stopover for refueling and exchange. Territorial concessions to Britain for oil exploration also increased air and sea traffic in and out of the Creek.[7]

Revenue from oil concessions and aviation went directly to the ruler, and this upset what had, up to this point, been the de facto power agreement between the ruler and a strong merchant class. While several reformist rumblings sprang up over the next few decades, no great upheaval occurred. Merchants were forced to find other sectors for business opportunities, both legal and illicit. Beginning in the 1950s, gold became the new resource to replace pearls in Dubai. While Kuwait had previously been the principal exporter of gold to India, the gold trade began shifting to Dubai because of its geographical location and economic growth. The British Bank of the Middle East in Dubai, for instance, would offer free dollars for gold trade, even though Dubai was still part of the sterling region, and in this way, an unusual three-way exchange of currency and bullion trade emerged that generated profits of 300 percent or more.[8] With much the same vision and flexibility that was demonstrated in competition with Persia, Dubai again utilized a lax regulatory system and a willingness to encourage business to solidify its economic position. At the turn into the twentieth century, while the port was taking on increased international trade functions, Dubai was still a small fishing village of 10,000 people. The urban layout included three areas located around the mouth of the Creek: Deira, consisting of 1,600 houses and 350 suq shops; Al Shindagha, a residence of the ruling family that included 250 houses; and Dubai, the smallest of the settlement areas with 200 houses and 50 suq shops. In 1955, the total urban area was a modest 3.2 square kilometers, but this would soon change.[9]

MUNICIPAL PLANNING

Oil concessions and aviation brought greater traffic in and out of Dubai, and it was quickly apparent that the city would require a more elaborate infrastructure network, as well as a plan. The 1950s saw urban expansion channeled along the shores of the Creek. International corporations were attracted to Dubai through oil exploration initiatives, and multilevel office buildings in Deira began transforming the fishing town's physiognomy. In 1957, the Dubai municipality was established to coordinate the booming activity, and by 1959 the British company of Sir William Halcrow and Partners was contracted by the city to dredge the Creek and open it up to allow for heavier shipping capacity.[10] The Creek dredging also helped to establish a framework for urban planning in Dubai, which would change in scale and scope over time but remain a blueprint for near-future urban development. Private investment and international loans from Britain, Kuwait, and Oman, largely for infrastructure development, helped to increase the overall efficiency and productivity of the Creek area, although the main objective was to allow for heavier equipment to be unloaded for oil exploration and for the growing construction sector. The British architect John R. Harris began drafting Dubai's first master plan in 1959, laying out a basic road structure and infrastructural plan that would be followed closely and completed throughout the 1960s. Almost simultaneously a land law was passed in 1960, determining how land throughout Dubai could be registered, regulated, and transferred. The Crown Prince Sheikh Maktum bin Rashid Al Maktum headed the land regulation committee, along with technicians from the Sudan, and established a system that essentially granted existing homesteaders, up to 1960, the rights to their properties. Any land unclaimed in the process would then fall under the ownership of the ruler, who could either sell or award it as he desired. An important element of the land regulation also required the municipality to pay any landowner market value for their property, if the land was required for municipal purposes.[11]

With these planning and land regulations in place, the Dubai municipality saw the strategic opportunity to reclaim land on the Deira side of the Creek by using what was removed from the dredging project. This reclaimed land then became the corridor for office, hotel, and municipal development, which the municipality was in turn able to either lease or sell without having to buy out any existing landowner plots within Deira—one of the densest parts of the city. In 1986, in his foundational *The Dubai Handbook,* Erhard Gabriel writes about the Deira development:

> During the past 20 years, about 50 high-rise buildings including hotels, banks, public services, company offices and shopping arcades were erected in the Bani Yas Road along the Creek and in the parallel road one block inland... On the ground floors of these high-rise buildings are exclusive shops and elegant shopping arcades. Above these are two or three floors of offices, followed by up to five floors of apartments. This unusual vertical combination of residential and commercial activity within one building, together with hotels, entertainment, restaurants and offices, ensures the area remains lively night and day.[12]

In effect, the southward development along the Creek on this reclaimed land became the city's central business district, and the vertical programmatic diversity of the buildings, particularly as described by Gabriel, reinforced a kind of interchangeability and repetition among them. The land was reclaimed as an infrastructural surface on which to build this new urban corridor, and after the first building demonstrated success with vertical mixed-use, the prototype was simply replicated with limited variation in form, height, and function. All in all, this development also conformed to Harris's 1960 plan.

Year	No. of Tankers	Export in barrels	Revenue in US$
1969	12	3,561,094	376,114
1970	79	30,949,134	11,556,000
1971	98	45,323,357	37,587,000
1972	110	55,595,650	54,128,000
1973	153	81,151,245	108,536,000
1974	146	88,317,655	558,042,000
1975	123	91,635,272	600,000,000

*Estimate

Dubai's crude oil exports and revenue, 1969–1975
Source: Al-Otaiba, M.S. *Petroleum and the Economy of the United Arab Emirates*. London: Croom Helm, 1977.

Dubai Population in '000s

1990	1939	1968	1975	1980	1985	1990	1995	2000	2005	2010
11	21	59	183	276	371	490	689	862	1,32	1,87

Dubai population from 1900 through 2010.
Source: Dubai: Statistic Center. www.dsc.gov.ae

In 1971, prompted by further economic growth and urbanization, Harris was commissioned, again, to produce a second plan for Dubai. In keeping with the times, he established a ring-radial road system, connecting the city's outer housing developments with the center city. The residential developments varied in social and ethnic composition, and many were originally designed as permanent housing for the traditionally nomadic Bedouin population of the emirate. Prototypical housing block groups, such as Al Awir and Lisayli, were built in the late 1970s, and the uniform plot sizes of 10,000 square feet corresponded to the amount of land Imarati received from the government on which to build their houses.[13] As was the case with Deira, the housing settlements varied slightly in design, social composition, and size, but the striking similarity of these residential areas, seems to follow prototypical designs that, once tested, were replicated in all subsequent government housing developments. Some of these residential compounds on the then periphery now house temporary service workers who work principally in the hotel industry. The plots are geometrically consistent and have a striking resemblance to the former agricultural plots that occupied Jumeira in the 1960s.

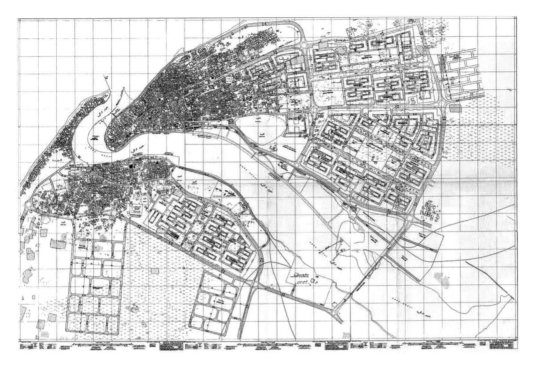

Dubai Town Plan (1960) by John R. Harris and Partners

FEDERATION AND TRANSITION

After fruitless oil exploration from the 1930s until the end of the 1950s, the British finally handed back their oil concession rights to Dubai. Shortly thereafter, the Dubai Petroleum Company struck "black gold" in 1966 in an area christened the "Fateh field," in what was to become one of four offshore fields with modest though significant reserves, which began exporting in 1969.[14] In 1968, the British announced a withdrawal of their interests in the Gulf, and in 1971, the seven independent sheikhdoms comprising the Trucial States federated into the United Arab Emirates.[15] At this time the seven sheikhdoms had a population of about 180,000 people, distributed across 90,600 square kilometers of mountain and desert, of which Dubai had a population of over 60,000 inhabitants but an area of only 4,114 square kilometers.[16] Federation effectively ended the treaty agreements with Britain and also coincided with the worldwide boosting of oil prices. Shortly before federation, Dubai began to adopt measures aimed at industrial diversification beyond oil and gas production.[17] The Dubai Cable Company was formed in 1979, along with the Dubai World Trade Center—a focal point of Middle Eastern business interest. Dubai Drydocks—a leading ship repairer—was also created at much the same time. The Dubai Aluminum Company was founded in the early 1980s, followed by incursions into leisure and tourism, including numerous shopping malls and Dubai Duty Free, dating from 1983.

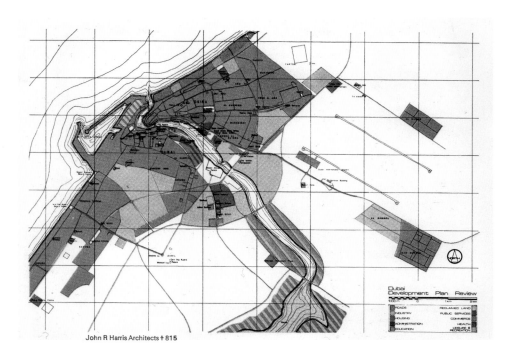

John R Harris Architects + 815

Dubai Second Town Plan (1971) by John R. Harris and Partners

More recently, further diversification has occurred, with Dubai Internet City and Dubai Media City. Having managed the largest *sukuk* market, Dubai became a regional hub for Islamic banking and finance, and subsequently expanded into an international financial center.[18] Much of this diversification was initiated with government funding and also included two major port facilities that proved to be the major boon to Dubai's reexport business and one of its chief sources of livelihood. Today this trade extends to over 120 countries, accounts for more than 20 percent of the UAE's gross domestic product, and incorporates the purpose-built Cargo Village, which opened at Dubai International Airport in 1991 as one of the world's leading air-cargo centers.[19] Free-trade policy was also boosted in 1985, when the customs directors of the Arab Gulf Co-operation Council (GCC) abolished the double taxation of goods reexported from a member nation. When implemented in Dubai in 1987, markets opened appreciably across the region and strengthened transshipment to elsewhere in the world.[20]

Port Rashid was built as a modern port facility at the mouth of the Khor Dubai Creek, which essentially updated the industrial functions of a reclaimed area west of the Creek's mouth. Creek trade would continue, though principally consisting of smaller trade from neighboring Gulf towns and Iran, as is still true today. In fact, although dwindling significantly, *dhow* traffic was responsible for two-thirds of Dubai's imports for reexport in the 1970s.[21] Port Rashid, however, soon proved to be insufficient for Dubai's export requirements. As a consequence, hundreds of ships had to wait for months off the coast for a chance to berth, and this hindered trade.

By 1976, planning began for the new Jebel Ali industrial port and logistics site 22 miles (35 kilometers) down the coast toward Abu Dhabi. The site would have the capacity to accommodate present and future industrial trade and logistic needs, while the other ports assumed smaller trade functions. The new port was to be the largest port-dredging project to date, and its scale and location broke strongly with the ring-radial morphology that Harris had designed in Dubai's second master plan.[22] Neighboring Saudi Arabia had begun plans the previous year on the two new industrial towns of Jubail and Yanbu, where the former was to serve as a massive port and industrial complex for Saudi oil export on its Gulf Coast. Both state-of-the-art facilities at the time, the Jebel Ali project closely resembled the neighboring Jubail project, and although Jubail entered the Guinness Book of World Records in 1983 as the largest man-made port-dredging project, it would not be long until the extension of Jebel Ali's facilities earned it this title.[23] In 1991, Port Rashid and Jebel Ali were combined under one administrative body and in 2001 merged with other authorities to form the Ports, Customs, and Free Zone Corporation (PCFC).[24] Quickly becoming the region's leading port operation, its container throughput in 2005, for instance, totaled a massive 7.62 million TEUs.[25] In 2006, all of these components were folded into an overarching holding company called "Dubai World," which essentially added other transportation, logistics, light industrial activities, and real estate components to PCFC.

CONTEMPORARY DEVELOPMENT

With the establishment of the Jebel Ali Port, Free Zone, and logistics center, connected back to the older city by Sheikh Zayed Road—now well and truly a modern expressway—Dubai broke with its past municipal plans by Harris, even as they were closely followed, at least as far as they went. Indeed, after 1980 the municipality contracted more than twenty master plans, including one by the Doxiades Office in Athens.[26] This approach, however, proved to be impractical given the new scale and rapidity of urban development. Instead, Dubai's subsequent urbanization appears to have followed a rather basic yet robust pattern. Within this scheme, a broadly spaced network of major roads and related infrastructure improvements took shape, opening up real estate largely for large-scale though diversified development—the mosaics mentioned earlier. This roadway network was anchored by at least three major connectors, running parallel to the coast, including Al Jumeirah Road, Sheikh Zayed Road, and the Emirates Ring Road, further inland. Within this framework, bands and broad zones of particular development emerged, each conforming, more or less, to locational advantages, within the broad infrastructure network, and more specific geographic characteristics. Consequently, much of the coastal zone—except for the ports—has been and is being used for water-oriented leisure and recreation facilities, including the bulk of related shopping opportunities and malls. Further inland, along Sheikh Zayed Road, especially toward older development along the Creek forming outward extremities of Harris's plans, high-rise commercial development sprang up, starting with the Dubai World

The Creek from the opposite side (Shindagah) showing the Deira skyline, with high-rise buildings built on reclaimed land

Trade Center of 1979. This development has taken place across the Creek from the earlier Deira Central Business District.

Up to 1979, the 650-foot tower block of the Trade Center was the tallest building in the Middle East, but was eventually eclipsed by the Burj Khalifa, further down the road toward Jebel Ali—now the tallest building in the world. In between are high-rise hotels, the Emirates Towers, and the Dubai International Financial Center. Both in theory and in practice, this spine of very high-rise building seems likely to continue along the expressway toward Jebel Ali. Still further inland and in a swath dividing the otherwise banded linear pattern of development were to be a sequence of extensive projects, each with a thematic focus (Dubailand, Sports City, Global Villages, etc.). Also inland and connected to the Ring Road, sweeping back up to Sheikh Zayed Road, are International City, Jumeriah Golf Estate and Village, and The Gardens. Zones in between the finer-grained coastal developments, as well as the massive Dubai Marina and Sheikh Zayed Road's skyscraper spine, and between this spine and the more extensive developments bordering the inland open desert, play host predominantly to what are locally referred to as "G + 1 housing"—a form of two-story villa developments analogous to those mentioned earlier in conjunction with Imarati land rights.

Originally peculiar to Dubai, although later emulated elsewhere in the Gulf area, land reclamation projects along the coast in the form of the Palm Jumeirah, The World, the Palm Jebel Ali, The Palm Deira, and portions of the huge future Dubai Waterfront development captured international media attention. Although exotic in shape—at least when viewed from the air—the projects sought to make rational use of the constant stream of dredge spoils produced

Aerial view of G+1 housing

nearby to keep the sea lanes open. They also effectively expanded the length of prized shoreline development.[27] Other major infrastructure projects included construction of the large Arabian Canal, extending in a loop from well on the other side of Jebel Ali, adjacent to the proposed Dubai Waterfront and the border with Abu Dhabi, inland and around to meet the coast again near the Palm Jumeirah, as well as the projected canaliza-tion from the Creek's wildlife headwaters through to the coast, past Burj Khalifa. Then too, there was the construction of mass-transit links of the Dubai Metro, down Sheikh Zayed Road and the adjacent inland thoroughfare, which makes good use of the density of development that is already substantial along this urban spine. The future also holds the filled-out prospect of the Al Maktoum International Airport and associated devel-opment purported to be roughly the scale of Heathrow, London, and O'Hare, Chicago, combined.[27] In short, much of the overall layout, or physical planning, of what still may

become the future city of Dubai has transpired through the designation of broad territories for focused, though loosely framed, real-estate development purposes, supported
by major, if not colossal, infrastructural improvements and locational parameters that
make general geographic sense.

Both within and between the broad elements of this emerging spatial framework,
another process that enhanced both the flexibility and speed of Dubai's urban production were the prototyping and replication mentioned earlier. One of the advantages
of prototypes, in this context, is that they offer a direction that can be tested and
followed, with a corresponding lowering of future knowledge costs and ease of replication. Another advantage is the considerable room allowed for specific articulation
within the overall outlines of the prototype itself. A tall tower is just that, allowing sufficient amplitude for considerable exploration of more detailed matters of shape and
appearance, as is a coastal land reclamation in a natural-looking or geomorphic form, or
a hotel complex having a distinctive form and thematic reference. Further, within broad
limits, dimensional amplification of the prototype appears to also be possible, judging
from the rise from the Dubai World Trade Center, to Burj Khalifa, mentioned earlier, or
the possibility of future, more extensively exotically shaped land-reclamation projects.
Indeed, such a process was in play, evidenced, among other projects, by the rough
replication—although at a vastly expanded scale of the existing "central" area development (including Port Rashid, the Creek, and the Sheikh Zayed Road high-spine) and
the proposed Dubai World Central area embracing the Jebel Ali Port, the Al-Maktoum
International Airport, and the Dubai Waterfront next to Abu Dhabi—at the other end of
the coast from Deira and the border with Sharjah. Many of the basic ingredients, so to
speak, are the same, although the ambition is orders of magnitude higher. In addition,
when both the number of significantly different territories—the band zones and mosaics described earlier—and the buildings or development types filling out each territory
remain relatively few, as they now do in Dubai, the urban territory can assume a rather
immediate legibility, even if it can lose out in complexity at a more detailed level, or
await that complexity through further stages of redevelopment. Finally, replication of
successful prototypes, in addition to lowering the knowledge costs of development,
may also be less risky, especially in what appears to be a supply-side-driven real-estate
market responding to high, though general and, therefore, shapeable demands.

One cautionary note on amplification arises, however, as structures become
higher, longer, and bigger, sometimes seemingly for the sake of it. What can result is
a means-end confusion, where means go in search of ends, rather than the other way
around. By contrast, to remain rational, as many have in the past, the means (i.e., longer,
higher structures) must be necessary, if not sufficient, to their ends.

And another note: More recent forays into high-end real-estate development
through land reclamation and the creation of artificial islands also borrows, replicates,
and amplifies infrastructure from Dubai's own specific past. The "fronds" of the Palm
projects bear specific resemblance to the breakwater extensions of Port Rashid and
Jebel Ali, and the speckled "World" islands look like the preliminary phase of any land
reclamation project. Time demonstrates which kind of infrastructural development

is more resilient. The point being that within a bundled possibility of infrastructural elements from which to choose to replicate and/or amplify, a city can potentially chose *incorrectly*, as may end up being the case for the island experiments. The island projects provide an exaggerated example, but whether because of the dangers of temporal obsolescence, or an overemphasis placed on certain infrastructure because of an unusual fad or trend, the correct selection of enduring infrastructure continues to involve an element of risk.

In summary, then, recent physical development of Dubai closely reflected free-trading and unconstraining attitudes practiced in other sectors. It was strongly driven by perceptions of external markets and Dubai's emerging position in the global interchange of goods, services, and personnel. After all, the Emirate has a low indigenous population relative to the size of its economic achievements and future ambitions, and could no longer rely on its modest natural resources for growth. Taking advantage of its location as a geographic point of transshipment within its region and beyond, Dubai manifoldly increased the significance of this advantage, through expanding infrastructure development to the point that it has become a major hub in a variety of international flows of goods and services. Primarily through a relatively loose arrangement of broad areas of development, linked by equally broadly defined elements of infrastructure, rather than through the potential constraints of conventional master planning, the urban territory of Dubai took fuller shape, expanding rapidly over the past decade. Although seemingly attention-grabbing in many respects, such as the world's tallest building, the only man-made features other than the Great Wall of China that can be seen from space, and the exotica of ski slopes in the desert, as well as strongly themed urban settlements, the underlying development logic, to a point, remained eminently rational. It attracted considerable amounts of international capital, took advantage of what there is of a geography and the locational advantages of an expanding urban infrastructure, and traded well on its image as a progressive place to be in the region. A relatively straightforward process of physical development, testing, and replication, at both small and large scales, also enabled Dubai to develop quickly by narrowing risk, decreasing the knowledge costs associated with further development, allowing for more specific articulation within the broad outlines of a particular type and the beginnings of an immediately legible urban landscape. In many respects, however, although Dubai's rise to wide international prominence among many audiences was new in coming, it was well positioned by earlier and sustained governmental decisions made around the time of federation into the United Arab Emirates, not the least of which was economic diversification, first around its reexporting and related industrial prowess, then into commercial services, leisure, and recreation, to be followed, more recently, by a full-blown financial market and entries into the knowledge business. What the future holds or how long Dubai's present relative dormancy will last remains to be seen. Meanwhile its urban development over the past half-century remains an extraordinary and eye-catching phenomenon.

Notes

1   Population statistics from various sources includ-
    ing Michael Pacione, "City Profile: Dubai," *Cities*, vol.
    22, no. 3, 2005, pp. 255–265; Erhard Gabriel, ed., *The
    Dubai Handbook* (Ahrensburg: Institute for Applied
    Economic Geography, 1987); the Municipality of
    Dubai; and Khaled Kassar, ed., *Why Dubai: 1000
    Numbers and Reasons* (Beirut: Beirut Information
    and Studies Center, 2006), p. 204.

2   R. Owen, "Cities of the Persian Gulf: Past, Present,
    and Future," lecture delivered at the University of
    Nicosia, Nicosia, Cyprus, October, 14, 2008.

3   Frauke Heard-Bey, *From Trucial States to United
    Arab Emirates* (London, New York: Longman, 1982,
    1997), p. 164.

4   Fatma Al-Sayegh, "Merchants' Role in a Changing
    Society: The Case of Dubai, 1900–90," *Middle Eastern
    Studies*, vol. 34, no. 1, January 1998.

5   Ian Fairservice, ed., *Dubai: Gateway to the Gulf*
    (London: Motivate Publishing, 2002), p. 23.

6   Gabriel, *The Dubai Handbook*, p. 71.

7   Ibid., p. 152.

8   Ibid., p. 142.

9   Heard-Bey, *From Trucial States to United Arab
    Emirates*, pp. 242–246.

10 Ibid., p. 258.

11 Gabriel, *The Dubai Handbook,* pp. 105–107.

12 Ibid., p. 105.

13 Ibid., pp. 107–108.

14 Fairservice, *Dubai,* p. 37.

15 Ibid., p. 9.

16 Ibid.

17 Ibid., p. 37.

18 Kassar, *Why Dubai*, pp. 167f, 81f , and 133f.

19 Ibid., p. 168.

20 Fairservice, *Dubai,* pp. 28–29.

21 Ibid., p. 29.

22 Stephen Ramos, *Dubai Amplified: The Engineer-
    ing of a Port Geography* (Farnham, Surrey, Eng-
    land; Burlington, VT: Ashgate, 2010).

23 Korea Development Institute, *Manpower
    Development Master Plan for Jubail and Yanbu,*
    Royal Commission for Jubail and Yanbu, Kingdom
    of Saudi Arabia; Seoul, 1980.

24 Fairservice, *Dubai,* p. 27.

25 Kassar, *Why Dubai*, p. 165.

26 Fairservice, *Dubai,* p. 35.

27 Kassar, *Why Dubai*, p. 116.

AMALE ANDRAOS
AND DAN WOOD

3

PEAK URBANISM, MICRO-PLANNING, AND OTHER EMERGENT REALITIES IN DUBAI

As if to parallel Dubai's exponential growth, recent years have witnessed a plethora of conferences, lectures, articles, and design studios that have chosen the young emirate as their focus. Our celebrity-obsessed culture has seemingly extended stardom to cities: every move is scrutinized, recorded, dissected, and replayed, rendering Dubai a site of both fantasies and anxieties. Either hailed as the prodigy city-state, model for the twenty-first century, or condemned as the terminal condition of the "city," where life has been reduced to its consumable image, Dubai seems fated to be evaluated in these opposite terms. While its detractors reduce Dubai to a hybrid of Las Vegas and Singapore—a soulless, merciless, and substanceless theme park—its fans applaud its extraordinary vision and boldness, unburdened by history and inert bureaucracy (let alone democracy), and hail Dubai as the ultimate site of groundbreaking new forms of urbanism.

This polarized debate misses much that is interesting or urgent about the questions that Dubai raises, questions about the future of cities, lifestyle, and power, as well as spectacle, the environment, segregation, the status of public space, and the possibility of public representation in the twenty-first-century city. Any attempt at conclusive remarks seems to fall short of the city's reality. For it is precisely the two most analyzed aspects of Dubai's urbanization, its image and its speed, that undermine any one-dimensional reading. Dubai's image is constantly recast to meet new desires, and the speed of its development outruns critique. As soon as a problem arises, Dubai produces the necessary remedy to protect its reputation.

One way to read the city today may be simply to capture the strange, unexpected, and often difficult reality that parallels the mythical world of Dubai and is most visible in the gaps between the announced, the planned, and the built. Two avenues are suggested by this reality: first, the possibility of reimagining new sequences of development, of rethinking urban relationships and reinventing typologies; and second, the confirmation that even the most perfectly constructed, controlled, and implemented vision is subject to unexpected forces—that of the economy, of course, but also those of building, of the desert, of density, and of a population whose shifting makeup, unstable desires, and maybe even discontent will determine much of Dubai's future.

Page 34-35: Sheikh Zayed Road, image and reality

RETHINKING THE URBANIZATION SEQUENCE: START WITH THE END

To launch its development and urbanization frenzy, Dubai adopted the iconography of modernism while reinventing its traditional sequence of implementation. With the building of Burj al-Arab in 1999, Dubai began to represent itself as a "world-class city"; at the same time it disposed of the burdensome old rules of master planning, zoning, and the building of infrastructure. Soon a series of iconic buildings, such as the twin-like Emirates Towers, the sail-like Jumeirah Beach Hotel, the various Media and Internet "Cities," and the Dubai Marina skyline, emerged from the desert. Jump-starting its development by boasting an instantly glamorous image, the thriving city-state attracted investors from around the globe. Savvy business populations moved in, and the legend of Dubai was born. This reliance on "design," vision, and narrative (i.e., theming) to start building the city was a principal characteristic of Dubai's development.

PEAK URBANISM

Transferring this strategy to the scale of the city, Dubai developed "peak urbanism": a city of intense physical nodes—islands with almost no connecting tissue. Random outbursts of hyperconcentrated vertical density rise from the flat desert landscape, creating an uneven skyline visible from miles away. The peaks do not only occur vertically against the horizon; they are also visible from outer space. Peak urbanism concentrates zones of intense activity, usually in the form of private, clearly bounded, and themed developments, and leaves the space in between to be filled with a low-rise combination of residential villas, dirt roads, and small-scale commercial activities.

The financial success of peak urbanism demands that the peaks achieve great density and a manufactured "difference" within. In an unintended side effect, this density creates sprawl elsewhere; previously amorphous neighborhoods such as Jumeirah, the residential area of choice for the local and expatriate elite, become welcome zones of release from the overly dense, overly planned, and overly themed. In a strange inversion, the excessive difference, specificity, and "extraordinariness" of the new developments flatten their space into generic sameness, while the contained zones of suburban sprawl become specific, refreshing islands of unself-conscious sand-colored villas, local supermarkets, offices, and even the occasional pedestrian.

MICRO-PLANNING

Peak urbanism's islands—"cities" and "villages," as they are called in the local idiom—are the key ingredients in Dubai's fast-track development. Rather than relying on heavy infrastructure and the time usually required to implement comprehensive master plans, Dubai has developed the technique of micro-planning. Each island/peak is both a destination and a hub: a city within a city where all necessary amenities, such as living, shopping, and dining, are provided. Like kiosks in an airport, the islands look different

Peak urbanism

but provide exactly the same amenities to a transient population. For the airport, transience is measured in hours; for Dubai's population of "guests," it is measured in weeks, months, or years.

The conventional and often nostalgic idea of the "city" is that of a layered site transformed by generations of human events; this new city's elements, more like islands than layers, are artificially manufactured in a controlled and conditioned environment that allows them to develop simultaneously at an accelerated rate. Each island is connected to the next by how long it takes to drive between them (which these days is a long time in heavy traffic).

The city's developers, driven by economics, rely heavily on theming as the sound-bite substitute for public space or programming. In this way, they are able to generate immediate, global, and mass-consumable meaning. It is not difficult, however, to imagine the potential of micro-planning, given a slightly enlarged focus. Allowing one to examine different urban and architectural typologies in parallel, micro-plans could reopen the "best of" utopian discourses without the totalitarian implications that led to their demise. Dubai could become a laboratory of ideas about urban life and especially about a smarter relationship with the environment.

After relying almost exclusively on big corporate design firms to generate hype and instant "modernity," Dubai is now inviting signature architects to research its past, analyze its present, and design its future. Yet this alliance of power and design still falls short of expectations. It is clear that Dubai's governing elite's embrace of "world-class architecture" is merely another global PR opportunity, making it difficult to imagine how effective change in the city's agenda, process, and form can happen.

INFRASTRUCTURE?

Dubai's infrastructure sits at the intersection of the city's successes and failures. As a result of reshuffling the development sequence, infrastructure has occupied a distant secondary place. While urbanization focused on intense but disparate self-contained private developments, each boasting a scientifically computed number of traffic lanes, parking lots, and bridges, no measure was taken to provide adequate support between these developments, leaving the already meager public realm underdeveloped and overburdened.

This secondary status has come back to haunt the city. The young emirate has developed one of the most serious cases of traffic congestion in the world, almost as if the city itself had discovered a natural way to regulate its speed. In September 2006, the Dubai English-language daily *Gulf News* announced that school children spent an average of four hours in traffic every day, compared to six hours in class. New developments such as the Jumeirah Beach Residence in Dubai Marina, the largest single-phase residential and commercial project in the world, will add up to 25,000 residents within a year with no new infrastructure in sight, whether in the form of roads or of public transportation.[1] With a population that is expected to triple in the next ten years,[2] Dubai is finally awakening to the need for shared networks and is launching plans for new roads, highways, underground metro lines, and a series of above-ground bus routes and light-rail trains. The most surreal expression of this absence of infrastructure is in the special areas of the city where land is reserved for all Imarati males who, upon turning twenty-one, are given 10,000-square-foot plots on which to build homes. In such areas, houses emerge from the sand, in an unmediated relationship to the desert.

If Dubai's development, fueled by public-private consortiums or private investments alone, is any indication of where urbanization in the early twenty-first century is heading, then infrastructure and shared amenities are urban species on the verge of extinction. They have not received a fraction of the attention enjoyed by the other, more lucrative aspects of urban life. Whereas sleeping, dining, shopping, working, and leisure have all been rethought, redesigned, and repackaged, transportation has not, but still relies on the rather antiquated industrial-age technology of the car. It is not uncommon for families to own three cars, and although there are public buses, the most visible forms of mass transportation are the privately owned buses that move the city's construction workers en masse from their camps to construction sites and back.

Although new roads are finally getting built, this retroactive step seems, to readapt a local coinage much favored by the elite, "un-visionary"—akin to building cable lines for stationary phones in our wireless era. Roads and highways cannot, however, alleviate traffic congestion unless there is a significant detachment from the car. Yet it is hard to imagine chic Imarati women, let alone their privileged European counterparts, the so-called Jumeirah Janes, hopping onto the new light-rail system. Clearly the city's density and ability to implement new projects make Dubai a prime candidate for rethinking transportation and shared infrastructure in general. Weaning itself off of the car would set an example for the region, and perhaps the world, and would elevate Dubai's standing in relation to the Imarati federal capital, Abu Dhabi.

Top: Young Imarati housing area
Bottom: Palm Island monumental axis

U-TURN PLANNING, OR THE FLEXIBILITY OF SPEED

Dubai's limited number of roads have been organized on the U-turn premise. Most have been laid out with a generous median, sometimes planted with palm trees, sometimes edged with decorative fencing to dissuade pedestrians from crossing. The median does not allow for left-hand turns, forcing drivers to continue past their destination, often for great distances, until an opportunity to make a U-turn presents itself. The U-turn is not an occasional convenience; it is the only way to get to one's destination. It is legal and encouraged.

Often, it is only after a series of wider and longer right turns, including extended forays into the desert, that a U-turn is finally made possible. By making each turn appear logical, an hour and a half is easily spent before reaching one's relatively nearby destination. The U-turn mentality is even carried to the airport, where a flight departing from the farthest gate is often asked to head back across the entire terminal to its assigned runway. Simply put, if you want to get somewhere in Dubai, you have to go past it, turn around, and come back again.

The U-turn phenomenon is a good analogy for Dubai's headlong growth and its general modus operandi. The lack of infrastructure, the snarling traffic jams, and the speculative frenzy in apartment sales all indicate that Dubai has moved faster and farther than it needed to, and a process of U-turning can now be seen in a number of areas. An interesting case is that of the Palm Jumeira. Having come to the realization that the Palm's housing density is overshadowing its marketed luxury, the developer, Nakheel, has begun redesigning the remaining "fronds" even as they market them to investors.

Might U-turn planning be a key to new ways of growing, one that adopts a more process-oriented planning ethos that allows for a frenetic pace of change and shows the ability to reverse direction while moving forward? Maybe, but U-turn planning may also be no model at all. It might simply be a privilege of wealthier states, which either have the luxury of dispensing with serious planning or the confidence that they can easily survive the consequences of not having planned.

CONTROL

In their desire to create a thriving city from dust, Dubai's leaders have tried to plan, project, and invent everything, with the declared ambition to leave no room for chance encounters. Experiences are designed within the tight confines of overarching themes, and lifestyles are marketed within the boundaries of gated communities. The feeling of overarching control is amplified by the fact that, given the intense desert heat, there is little outdoor life possible for at least six months of the year, and what there is largely takes place within hotels and gated "cities" and "villages." The rest of the public realm is found in publicly accessible private interior space, from interior streets in shopping malls to hotel-hosted leisure, dining, and entertainment.[3] One moves from the private space of a car to the private space of a mall or an office park to the private space of a hotel. Only the older streets still provide the feeling of public mingling, as pedestrians

Behind the scenes

head to the mosques, churches, and temples, or to old markets, walking through the sinuous human-scaled streets that do not belong to any "city-within-the-city" but to the city of Dubai itself.

Control does not manifest itself only at an urban level, for the culture's codes of conduct are all intimately linked to issues of private and public space. Many, though by no means all, Muslim women wear the *hijab* (head covering), or even the veil, to extend their private space within the public realm, enabling them to move everywhere while feeling protected. While appearing unveiled and unaccompanied in the open-air public streets is seen by many Muslim women as dangerous to their reputation (*sum'a* in Arabic) for respectable behavior,[4] these women feel comfortable walking uncovered and alone in malls privately owned by Imarati families and corporations. In the latter spaces gates, guards, and camera surveillance are seen, somewhat ironically, to extend private, and therefore, permissible, space. Similarly, alcohol consumption, strongly frowned upon by Islam, often happens in Dubai within private spaces, especially in the city's resort hotels.

By extending private space into the city, many of these codes find an enlarged territory, expanding the spectrum of freedoms (contrary to generally accepted Western notions, where privatization of public spaces is almost always understood as loss of freedom). Yet this effect is only superficial: behind the illusion of increased mobility, these imported Western models of urban privatization and gentrification are actually working together with traditional Muslim codes of control, making them highly desirable and easily implemented. Control is a fundamental aspect of Dubai's success: without a unified vision that has no room for political disturbance, Dubai would not have been able to sustain a boom that brought together a mix of money from many sources and a highly diverse immigrant population.

REINVENTED TYPOLOGIES AND STYLES: THE HIGHWAY BOULEVARD

Dubai has developed a number of fascinating new architectural and urban typologies and hybrids that are influencing the region and beyond. The most notable, perhaps, is the highway boulevard: an evolution of the tower-in-the-park, extended to the parkway. Perfected by the endless stretch of Sheikh Zayed Road, the highway boulevard not only functionally combines two traditionally polarized experiences, it also combines them symbolically: the high-speed multilane road for cars as symbol of modernity, and the boulevard as classical representation of power and order, making it the site of the most prestigious addresses for both commercial and residential uses. With this new symbolic quality, the highway boulevard has become a staple of new developments in both Dubai and the region. From the central axis of the Jumeirah Palm Island, to the new Mecca Western Gateway (a 10-kilometer high-speed highway/residential and commercial boulevard linking the Jeddah highway to the Haram, the sacred city), this new typology creates a hybrid between the suburban and the urban. Yet to combine the highway and the boulevard, Sheikh Zayed Road negates the pedestrian at ground level, reinforcing the impossibility of moving around outside of a private zone; the road's main distinction is now as a leading site of pedestrian deaths. To walk the road is something that happens briefly at drop-off areas, either carved from the ground floor of buildings or placed to the side, perpendicular to their main axes. Elevated within the towers, moving from one floor to another of breathtaking views, reaffirms that the city is best experienced from a distance, as an image.

THE NEW OLD

> Anyone who does not attempt to change the future will stay a captive of the past.
> —Sheikh Muhammed bin Rashid Al Maktum

The Burj Khalifa was marketed by EMAAR as a place where "the old meets the new," despite the "old" and the "new" being on completely parallel construction tracks. This "visionary" confusion between old and new is endemic; a recent winner of an online photography contest contrasted the modern forms of the Burj al-Arab, not an EMAAR project, though, like EMAAR, part of Sheikh Muhammad's business empire, with an old building whose roofscape featured a series of traditional wind towers. The only problem was that the wind towers were part of the Suq Madinat Jumeirah hotel complex, completed more than five years after the Burj al-Arab. While Sheikh Muhammed may not consider himself a captive of the past, many developments reach backward to complete the sheikh's vision of the future.

The most interesting outcome of this Old-New/New-Old phenomenon is the unique resonance style that is emerging. Resonance style is the style of the twenty-first century: it samples elements and motifs from sources as disparate as old Hollywood movies and archeological findings and combines them with flights of architectural fancy on the part of corporate designers whose sole task is to channel a vernacular that has never existed. The result is something reminiscent of the past that resonates with a public's nostalgic yearnings, yet clearly has just been invented. Resonance style has the added benefit that it need not sacrifice any modern amenity, including scale, in the performance of its programmatic and economic duties. With the unstoppable urbanization of every possible territory, resonance style bridges nothing to everything, providing an à la carte menu of references whose origins have long been made irrelevant. In Dubai, resonance style covers everything from modernist heroic references (e.g., the glass skyscraper) to arabesque-patterned façades.

REALITY TRUMPS IMAGE

With a significant fraction of the world's cranes busy in Dubai, the young emirate is becoming reality even faster than its billboards can announce what's new—a reality that is often different from these imagistic promises. First, there is the reality of building. Whereas Burj al-Arab is characterized by a certain kitsch and flimsiness that undermines its claims to being a "wonder of the world," recent construction features an unexpected permanence and seriousness. Dubai is building for the future, and the future still lies in the desert. It is not just building quality that has created this unexpected gravity; it is also the harshness of the environment. While models and renderings in sales offices or on billboards may sell the fantasy of a negated desert turned

Sheikh Zayed Road

lushly green, the desert and its even, hazy light renders buildings almost austere. The excess projected by the fantasy is needed to create this attractive "something out of nothing," yet the "nothing" is actually something real. The desert is so strong and present that no amount of water-sprinklered lawns will ever make it disappear. Ironically, the more building there is, the more desert and heat are generated. Because construction creates more and more "heat islands," foci of increased heat that result from hot air exhausted around air-conditioned spaces or reflected from hard asphalt surfaces, Dubai gets hotter the more it is trying to cool itself. These two seemingly opposed phenomena, excessive fantasy and excessive reality, come together and counteract each other in a strange balance that typifies the push and pull of a striving new urban center.

Second, there is the issue of Dubai's labor population. Also a result of the micro-planning strategy, much of the emirate's immigrant workforce—for example, those in the construction industry along with some service workers at shopping malls—live in labor camps far from the city proper. Comprising nearly 90 percent of the private-sector workforce in the UAE, they are denied basic rights such as freedom of association and the right to collective bargaining. Their meager salaries, often as low as $150/month, can go unpaid for long periods. With the loans that most foreign laborers have to take on to move to Dubai, the result is virtual debt bondage. Despite the threat of extradition, migrant workers have increasingly resorted to public protests and strikes in an attempt to improve working conditions. Government figures show that between May and December 2005, at least eight major strikes took place. One in November 2006 quickly spread from construction workers who rioted at one skyscraper to others working on a new airport terminal.[5] Such harsh conditions (described in more detail by Gharavi, this volume) are reminiscent of the gilded age of capitalism, with its laissez-faire indifference to the exploitative foundations of wealth production. Employer practices, however, underestimate the savviness of the guest workers: in recent years, construction workers have been allying with advocates to publicize their situation on websites such as "mafiwasta" ("no wealthy or influential connections" in Arabic) and have, through organizations such as Human Rights Watch, put the construction industry under a cold and unforgiving light. Global technologies are thus a two-edged sword: they provide the cheap labor on which Dubai is dependent, and they provide the means for increased visibility of the realities faced by laborers once in Dubai. With the construction boom feeding off its labor force, Dubai needs to find a solution to abuses, not only to preserve its image of modernity but also to protect its flourishing economy from the increasingly frequent strikes, work stoppages, and other disturbances.

A third issue complicating the relationship between image and reality is that of Dubai's projected density. The emirate has constructed a myth of a luxurious lifestyle to attract the middle class and the wealthy, but this constructed image risks undermining itself. With a population expected to triple in ten years, developments are planned to maximize profit by maximizing units. Like Kevin Mitchell, in this volume, we too worry that Dubai's micro-planning and inattention to urban design and sustainable planning will create a city that soon will be uninhabitable, chaotic, and dense. For Dubai to embody its "vision," it needs to attract people to fill its buildings. But when they are

Migrant workers

filled, there may be nothing left of the glitter and the themes, only the overwhelming experience of an overpopulated and congested place.

Finally, Dubai's reality is emerging with its population. It is often said derisively that the legendary lines of potential buyers at the opening of every development are composed largely of investors and speculators; the influx of immigrants is, in fact, steadily increasing. With the 2005 law linking property ownership to residency, over-turning the older law that made ownership dependent on nationality (a first for the Gulf region), Dubai finally allowed its expatriate population to consider the emirate a permanent home. A significant part of this population comes from the Middle East. With the current tensions between the Middle East and the West, a great deal of Arab and Iranian investment has been diverted to Dubai. It is not only second homes for wealthy Gulf nationals that constitute this market; these are primary residences as well. Every instability in the region prompts an influx of wealthy "refugees" or middle-class citizens of neighboring countries, such as Iraqis, Lebanese, and Palestinians, ready to build a new life and choosing Dubai as the place.

This change, combined with the commitment to Dubai as home for many other nationalities (Indians, British, etc.), is slowly transforming Dubai from a mere hub into a cosmopolitan city. Already signs are appearing: trendy art galleries and cafés are emerg-ing with the usual appropriation of industrial or warehouse-like buildings, Dubai's inter-national film festival has been launched, and more critical thinking about the city and its future is being heard. How these populations' pasts, educational backgrounds, income levels, and tastes influence the supply by changing the demand is still an open question.

In ten years, Dubai will have aged considerably. Will the city be glittery and fake? Will it be congested and impossible to live in, let alone navigate? Will it be empty and bankrupt? Indeed, since 2008, this frightening possibility seems less far-fetched. What will it look like and how will it function? Answers to these questions cannot be found today. Certainly it will need to adjust to survive: labor conditions cannot last as they are, civil liberties should develop, and so should a stronger endorsement of sustainable living and building. Most important, more serious thought should be given to the connection between urban development and speculation, as well as to an over-dependence on sectors of the economy vulnerable to financial cycles. But in a city where everyone seems to be involved in, or at least proud of, the city's building boom, it is hard to imagine that the young city-state will not recognize smarter ways to move forward.

Notes

1   Robert Ditcham, "Mega Projects Add to Congestion," *Gulf News*, August 21, 2006.

2   Speculation on population growth is in Dubai a matter of politics and a propaganda tool. As a result, it is difficult to find reliable sources. Government sources tend to be confident about the population's steady increase, while critics and NGOs seem overly conservative, given the expansion of the past five to ten years.

3   "Public" excludes the migrant laborer population, which is not allowed to move outside of its assigned spaces of living and working.

4   As Dubai has expanded over the last twenty to thirty years, and with more foreigners immigrating, many Imaratis feel that the city has gone from a "village" (*qarya*) to cosmopolitan "city" (*madina*). This transition has been accompanied by many associations, but among them is a distinct feeling that the city is becoming dangerous. It is within this context that codes of gender segregation, as a means of construing and maintaining acceptable social interaction, have become more salient.

5   This essay was written in late 2006–early 2007 and does not reflect more recent worker protests.

BORIS BRORMAN JENSEN

4

LEARNING FROM DUBAI:
IS IT POSSIBLE?

In this chapter, I describe the kinds of formal experimentation that are occurring in Dubai. Although even Las Vegas's teachable excesses can appear to pale in comparison to those of Dubai, a key to understanding the Gulf city lies in seeing how it partially cites and incorporates well-regarded planning and design traditions. It is this excessive citation and its amplification in terms of size, repetition, and class segregation that are Dubai's specific contribution to the current global urban landscape.

DYNAMICS OF BINGO URBANISM

Less than 10 percent of Dubai's gross national product derives from oil production, compared to 55 percent in 1980. One of the main reasons for this formidable shift in the economy is the massive investment that over recent decades has provided Dubai's desert land area with infrastructure and other site-development projects. Since independence at the beginning of the 1970s, the United Arab Emirates have spent $225 billion on expanding infrastructure.[1] Eight-lane motorways run through the desert and divide almost desolate areas into strategic plots. Pipelines connect enormous power plants to oil wells. Desalination plants with widely branched distribution systems and modern communication technologies form an open-plan structure of technological support along the Persian Gulf. Together with a rapidly increasing number of spectacular high-profile projects, infrastructure provides a unifying narrative for the city.

Urbanized Dubai comprises a rectangular system measuring roughly 500 square kilometers of irregularly built-up areas, which run along the coast from the frontier with the neighboring state of Sharjah in the north to Jebel Ali Port in the south. No original city center can effectively be said to exist (although, as Ramos and Rowe argue in this volume, the Creek can be seen as the effective traditional locus of a central business district of sorts). The majority of old buildings were demolished long ago, but the street array around the tidal inlet of the Creek has retained part of its concentric structure and has become a loose knot in an organic grid of north/southbound arteries and east/westbound connecting roads. As scattered urban development has taken place,

old buildings are demolished to make space for new ones and empty spaces are filled. Unsurprisingly, however, primary growth takes place within those areas left untouched by the infrastructural system, which despite a calculated overcapacity nevertheless requires regular expansion to absorb the increasing growth.

There has been an attempt to organize Dubai's urban development according to a traditional modern ideal. This has involved clear zoning and a rational organization of production in a finely woven network of mobility, which works according to some sort of "fuzzy functionalism" instead of Fordism's principle of assembly-line order.[2] Yet despite definitive planning for monofunctional areas of general, rectangular systems, the culture of construction that has emerged does not behave according to any known ideal. The scattered structure of growth oases does not match the concentric model, yet neither does it call to mind anything that can be traced back to the earlier autonomous enclaves of polycentric conurbations. Neither is this situation controlled by the formalistic principle of dispersion, which ribbon development immediately simulates. Dubai has a backbone of development along the coast, but all modern programs such as business parks, residential enclaves, shopping centers, and so on, which make up the greater part of urban growth, are too scattered to form a recognizable territorial pattern. The city is a fragmented post-polycentric environment held together by technologies with their base in mobility, whose general layout is a French landscape, but whose local organization complies with an English garden plan, and whose economic dynamic is globally oriented.

Page 48-49: Billboards showcasing prospects of Dubai
Opposite: The Sheikh Zayed Skyline seen from the outer ring road
Below: Immigrant construction workers near the Burj Dubai site

This combination of rational structure, autonomous internal organization, and external growth conditions makes Dubai a good representative of what California geographers Michael Dear and Steven Flusty have labelled "keno capitalism."[3] The system of infrastructure divides the uniform desert landscape, mechanistically, into numbered units like a bingo board. The incoherent private development projects descending from above are like pieces drawn in some external game with no relations of physical proximity. These conditions make the image of "the city as gaming board seem an especially appropriate twenty-first century successor to the concentrically ringed city of the early twentieth century."[4] With globalization, Dubai has come to evince this kind of "bingo urbanism," a mosaic of monocultures in a field of business opportunities.

The huge mass of structural imports that form the basis of Dubai's development were initiated and carried out by English engineering firms allowed to function as a kind of local authority in the first consolidation phase.[5] All public services such as sewage systems, electricity and water supply, and waste disposal were in the hands of a small number of private companies that came to play a central role in local affairs. The close connection between the state and a few handpicked companies is, however, largely a thing of the past. A locally based expatriate labor force has taken over the operation of the various facilities, a new system of tenders has partly replaced the more personal connections of earlier times, and the sheikhs' unit shares in several of the active consortiums have made the distinction between private corporations and state activities more diffuse.

Dubai's majority expatriate population has no formal civil rights. Theming can be seen to dramatize this lack by aesthetically overemphasizing the putative utopianism of global space. This is a "wonderland" of consumption, and tourism is one of the city's most important sources of income. Today, 25 percent of Dubai's GNP derives directly or indirectly from tourism. The number of visitors will, according to airport authorities, increase from the present 15 million to 45 million per year within the next three decades.[6] The thematic organization of space can, to a certain degree, control bingo urbanism's random pattern of expansion.

The most significant alteration to this global post-industrial city-state may be the introduction of the extensive enclaving that defines the city's places, coordinates the heterogeneity of space, and keeps the architectonic elements apart. This themed enclaving, moreover, has an afterglow of re-feudalization and therefore exceeds a poly-centric urban fragmentation in which each enclave as a decentralized unit contains the narrative of totality. Although Dubai's post-polycentric urban pattern is generally woven together by infrastructure and exclusively differentiated by theming and enclaving, the representation of the city as material culture has no indexical picture to which to refer. There is no stylistic discrepancy between, for example, the Egypt-

inspired entrance of the Wafi shopping center and the adjacent High-Tech residential tower. Postmodern citation has emancipated the continuity of history and pluralized the semantic logic.

THE CITY OF THE IMAGE

Two of Dubai's best-known monumental buildings are the Burj al-Arab luxury hotel and the Palm projects, three giant palm-tree-shaped peninsulas that will materialize in the next few years in Jebel Ali, Jumeirah, and Deira. These projects will feature entertainment and residential developments reserved for the wealthiest of global elites. Kevin Lynch's insights, made more than forty years ago about the image of the city, have thus come full-circle, and the themed, enclaved city has become the city of the image.

The Palm was created as an image and not planned as an actual project until the image had proved its conceptual strength. Without heavy marketing, the thousands of millionaires' residences would not have been sold, and without strict design precepts, The Palm would never resemble its original idea, its image. In this sense, architecture has become the last link in the semiotic chain that ties a cultural image to place and city. The Palm erodes all traditional contexts; there was nothing before The Palm, and its community, if it can indeed be called that, will fashion its attachment to place though the form of a brand.

The artificial landscapes off Dubai's coast may be expressions of an autonomous materiality in regard to the symbol, but The Palm refers primarily to its own nature and is therefore emblematic of the way in which habitat can be lifted out of its given otherness and shifted into a virtual ecology of conceptual projection. The role of the architect is to design within the style that has been predetermined by the design manual, actually a variation on a dizzying number of generic styles such as "Italian," "Mexican," and "Ranch." These thematized offerings signal a strategic alliance between the idea of a global jetset lifestyle and a generalized local style. Architecture as the articulation of a global focal plane has been on the program for a long time, no more clearly than in the International Style of modernism. What is new, however, is that the cultural expressions that are specific to a certain region have been drawn into this symbolic broadcasting as generic markers. Folklore has become "fakelore."[7]

HERITAGE PLANNING: IMPROVING THE PAST

Not only is Dubai's future taking shape at a rapid rate, but the city's past is also in a process of radical change. EMAAR Properties, the company that is building new golf communities and luxury enclaves in the Jumeirah district, is restoring the "old" Dubai around the tidal inlet's southern bank in Bur Dubai. From the Al Fahidi roundabout in the east and nearly 1,000 meters to the west, there will be a new and historically transformed urban area consisting of the Bastakiyya and al-Suq al-Kabir (the Large Market) districts. Here several historical fragments of isolated buildings and smaller built-up sections are scattered over a large area and hidden between modern developments.

As the name implies, there is a market in the area, but there is also a museum of national history and a small cluster of traditional buildings known as the Bastakiyya, named in memory of the quarter's original Iranian inhabitants, who came from a part of Iran called Bastak. Buildings in the Bastakiyya were erected in coral stone and constructed around confined courtyards, and equipped with the characteristic *barjeel*, cooling wind towers, which still jut out over the flat-topped roofs. The Bastakiyya district is being extended, and the number of historic-looking buildings will have grown considerably in the near future. A predetermined route through the area is the main control mechanism that will tie the districts to the narrative of the city, "particularly those areas which are relatively unchanged by the fast pace of development."[8] Parking is available by a nearby roundabout or at the Dubai Historical Museum, and the trip, which takes the visitor through the sixteen most important points in the thematically bound narrative of the city's history, is estimated to last two hours.

Opposite the eastern entrance of the museum is the "Ruler's Office," the so-called Diwan. The building is from 1990 but is built in the old style, with majestic cooling towers. There are also a few mosques in the area. The mosques are both visual urban landmarks and, becaue of the *athan* or Muslim call to prayer, an auditory feature in the experience of the city. When following the itinerary further, one is guided westward with pauses at strategic places, along the Ali ibn Abi-Taleb Street, past the textile suq, and further westward to a promenade that runs along the inlet. The next stop on the tour is the former ruler Sheikh Sa'id Al Maktum's residence in Shindagha. The Shindagha

The Diving City in Bur Dubai

quarter is not completed: none of the thirty-two original houses is restored yet, but "Dubai Municipality's plans [are] to restore the area to its former glory."[9]

Until then, the area where the inlet breaks and districts 311 and 312 converge will be dominated by the neighboring Carrefour supermarket and the stacked containers at Port Rashid. Without a narrative imposed by tour guides and the tourist's predisposition to find an "authentic history" in urban artifacts, such a transmogrification of existing urban space would simply be impracticable. The "old" Dubai we are presented is not an expression of a "true" past. The story related here serves as entertainment and has sidestepped the city's actual past. This does not mean that this particular story of the "old Dubai" is entirely without links to reality, but it illustrates what Anthony Giddens has described as modernity's separation of time and space and its use of history to make history, universalizing not only the future but also the past.[10]

JON JERDE WAS HERE: DUBAI FESTIVAL CITY

The fictionalization of space that influences the reconstruction of the "old" part of Dubai can be read through the lens of the "epic urban landscape," in which history is marketed, rearranging the city to satisfy the growing market for entertainment. Leisure time and the past have become parallel consumption domains, both significant as regards identity and therefore constituting an important twinned economic dynamic of the city. The loss of origins as myth and their reconstitution as commodity (or, as Marx might say, the conversion of history from use to exchange value) constitutes but one aspect of the ongoing retreat that here is being conducted by architecture. The reshuffling of space taking place in the Bastakiyya, Suq al-Kabir, and Shindagha districts bears witness to the ways in which this new economy has had an extra dimension added to its plan. In urbanism, event has largely replaced volume in significance. And where planning used to assume that life could be molded through the control of space, now it is apparently space that controls the market's organization of life as style.

The architect behind a striking urban development project in Dubai, the Dubai Festival City, is the Californian global place-maker Jon Jerde, and he expresses this paradigmatic twist in the social grammar of architecture: "Our curves are not formal, but perceptual; they are used to draw people in."[11] In much the same way as the optical illusions and anamorphoses of the baroque era attempted to burst the physical limits of space by capturing the attention of the spectator from a specific position, urban space is now controlled by a script that directs consumer toward constant consumption. The expansion of consumption economics is not limited by the physical dimensions of the city. Dubai Festival City is organized like a story, similar to reconstructed history in the shape of narrative. The architect treats space as a storyboard and regards urbanity as something that, first and foremost, extends in time. "Our work synthesizes many disciplines in order to produce the tools needed to advance human community as we move into time."[12] Jerde calls this space a "scripted space," and even the name underlines the festivalization of the city. "'The Disneyland effect' has entered our language, to remind us that hypertrophied mall 'cities' have become essential to globalized tourism."[13]

The chief executive officer of Festival City, American architect and businessman Lee Tabler, said "The Internet is an essential part of Dubai Festival City's communication with potential tenants and curious onlookers alike ... In many circumstances it is the first contact some people have with us and it is essential that the website present a dynamic, clear and consistent message."[14] The future success of the project depends on whether the laying of the electronic "foundations" is successful. The project will cover an area of about 500 hectares, stretching approximately 4 kilometers along the north side of the tidal creek from al-Garhoud Bridge in the east. The project has been given the status of "a city in the city," a description based on its size alone. This new city-in-the-city is will consist of fifteen districts targeting different groups, determined through market research. The plan is shaped like a tadpole. A 55-story tower constitutes the landmark of the Festival City and orients the development toward the west. A tail comprised of corbie-stepped buildings suggests the maritime theme of "waterfront development."

Jerde calls his strategy "place making," and one of its fixed reference points is classical town space such as we find in the historic city centers of northern Italy. "Place making" has to be understood in contrast to the European-dominated contextualism that attempts to express the inherent character of the place and an impression of its spirit, such as Christian Norberg-Schulz prescribes in his notion of genius loci.[15] Jerde is interested in historic styles as scripts and not as expressions of a place-specific character. Dubai Festival City is not bound to place as an expression of genius loci or any other embedded vernacular. Jerde himself delivers all the inscriptions, even those that refer to something historic. According to a press release, "when we looked at the site we found it had the right energy we were looking for, it was virgin land which gave us the flexibility to do what we wanted to do."[16]

Dubai Festival City thus has its origins in what can be called "genius logo," or town planning as media strategy. The plan is a brand; a loyal double of the project's logo. "The logo reflects the dynamism of Dubai Festival City and will assist in establishing its image with its local, regional and international audiences."[17]

The developer behind Dubai Festival City is the Al-Futtaim Group, which operates within a range of financial sectors and brands such as Volvo, Lexus, and IKEA. The Al-Futtaim Group has financed the project alone and therefore can lease the majority of its commercial programs itself. Once it is completed, this $4 billion development will be the largest mixed-use real estate project in the Middle East. The festival city will not be inhabited in the traditional sense of the word; it will be time-shared. Festival City is a consumption community, the inhabitants are consumers, the city is a store, and the recreational facilities form part of the development plan as effective production facilities. The eighteen-hole Robert Trent Jones II golf course, the "green" element in the development, is not just designated for fun; it is for the use of the elite's "business vacation©."[18] With Dubai Festival City, the Al-Futtaim Group has completed what mallification has long heralded but only hinted at realizing: the mall has actualized its latent ambition of assuming the character of a consummated city.

The prestigious Creekside Golf Club

GOLF AND THE *HABITATION ARMÉE*

At the top of the hierarchy of the desert state's green enclaves are golf courses, most notably the two eighteen-hole courses of Dubai Creek Golf and Emirates Golf Club. Dubai Creek Golf's clubhouse, with its contours in the shape of a fully rigged sail and prominent location at the waterfront of the inner harbor, has some references to Jørn Utzon's Opera House in Sydney. Both clubs' courses are ranked highly by the international golf community. At the same time as golf is conquering ever larger shares of the overall recreational landscape, several of the newest and most fashionable residential developments in Dubai have been built around greens and laid out as golf communities.

EMAAR Properties' "visionary community," The Greens, is a good example. According to the promotional literature, the twin aims of the Jumeirah district development are that it "meet the needs of your family and provide you with the prestige of being steps away from Emirates Golf Club."[19] Nearby, the 25 square kilometers of the Emirates Hills, also by EMAAR, boasts The Colin Montgomerie Golf Course Community. The development has its own golf course designed by "world champion golfer Colin Montgomerie," but the development itself is also shaped and characterized as a golf-like terrain. All of the large villas have a view of an artificial landscape whose topography and picturesque protective planting conform to the requirements of a professional golf community. Boundaries with the surrounding landscape as well as those between individual properties are camouflaged by areas of green plantation. The view from the inside suggests that the private domain is unlimited, but Emirates Hills is a restricted area: "for your comfort and peace of mind, we've made Emirates Hills a 'gated community', with restricted access and round-the-clock security."[20] Although there is virtually no crime in Dubai, according to available statistics, the militarization of the boundary with the surroundings is necessary to display to outsiders that the golf community has seceded from the surrounding city and society. The fence guarantees for its inhabitants the opportunity for "escape and tranquillity."[21] The modernists' dream of Unité d'Habitation has become *Habitation armée*, the fortified community.

SHEIKH ZAYED'S POTEMKIN CORRIDOR

The 3-kilometer stretch of Sheikh Zayed Road between the World Trade Center and the so-called military roundabout is the city's Little Manhattan. A single row of skyscrapers on each side of the eight-lane road symbolically graphs the city's towering economy and constitutes a sort of monumental town gate in the otherwise flat urban area. In addition to the 1970s-monolithic World Trade Center, the Potemkin corridor consists of several characteristic block tower developments, including the 300-meter Chicago-style twin Emirates Towers, the four-towered and neogothic Fairmont Hotel, and the much-

Sheikh Zayed Road seen from a parking lot

hyped Burj Dubai. From certain angles, the double row of tower blocks is an impressive manifestation of the powerful aesthetics of commerce, yet they appear more fragile when viewed from the surrounding post-industrial urban landscape, away from the tunnel effect.

This row of towers is a trademark of Dubai's high-profile economy and represents its central business district, but the symbol has also become a nostalgic echo of a time when it was still possible to measure a city's power by the height of its skyline. This image of the city was connected to an emerging industrialism, and the Dubai scenario almost caricatures the modernist vision of the city as a lucky coincidence of elevated engineering and scientific rationalism.[22] The tower block silhouette along Sheikh Zayed Road has already become a historic outlying quarter when seen in relation to the new agglomerations of network societies further down the same road.

LEARNING FROM DUBAI

The few examples I have described here provide sufficient documentation to destabilize basic assumptions in the theory of modern architectural and urban planning, both in quantitative and qualitative terms. The claim can be made, with *Learning from Las Vegas* in mind, that as macrohistoric phenomena, Dubai's extravagant projects are to globalized post-industrial society what "the Strip" was for "Main Street America." Dubai's urban development demonstrates how the globalized, post-industrial city takes on a "game board" character representing a form of bingo urbanism, with imported building capacity, themed landscape scenarios, and structures promoting mobility.

There is, however, another significant aspect to the story of Dubai that relates to the recirculation of all of these elements requisitioned from abroad. For although Dubai's extensive importation of everything from cheap labor to record-breaking architecture and urban planning might appear to be the city's Achilles' heel, it is also its strength. Just as Bilbao reinvented itself as a post-industrial metropolis by importing a Guggenheim museum, so Dubai, as "city of the image," is an example of how, given the new challenges to political identity posed by globalization, architecture and urban planning constantly have drawn from a cornucopia of universal possibilities to construct an identity.

Notes

The research for this chapter was made possible by grants from Statens Kunstfond and Ester og Jep Finks Fond Mindefond for Arkitektur og Kunsthåndværk. The Research Board at the AAA has funded the translation made by John Mason of Odense University. I am deeply indebted to Morten Daugaard, Mette Frisk Jensen, Ole B. Jensen, and Gitte Marling for insightful critique. Thanks also to Ahmed Kanna for his editorial efforts. All images by the author.

1   According to *Gulf News* online edition, November 11, 2001, www.gulfnews.com (accessed June 2, 2005).

2   In other words, a logic that does not follow a framework of scientific management. "Fuzzy functionalism" thus refers to the highly rational yet eccentric planning schemes used in Dubai.

3   See Michael Dear and Steven Flusty, "The Postmodern Urban Condition," *Spaces of Culture: City-Nation-World*, Mike Featherstone and Scott Lash, eds. (London: Sage, 1999), p. 77.

4   Ibid., p. 81.

5   See Gwilym Roberts and David Fowler, *Built on Oil* (Berkshire: Ithaca Press, 1995), p. 135.

6   According to Dubai International Airport's website, this number includes transit passengers, which makes the airport the world's sixth-fastest-growing and at the same time Dubai's most important shopping center. www.dubaiairport.com, accessed February 2003.

7   See Tracy Metz, *FUN: Leisure and Landscape* (Rotterdam: Nai Publishers, 2002), p. 177.

8   *Townwalk Explorer* (Dubai: Explorer Publishing, 2000).

9   Department of Tourism and Commerce Marketing project description of "Shindagha Cultural and Heritage Project," 2002.

10 "We can all sense how fundamental the separation of time from space is for the massive dynamism that modernity introduces into human social affairs. The phenomenon universalises that 'use of history to make history' so intrinsic to the processes that drive modern social life away from the hold of tradition. Such historicity becomes global in form with the creation of a standardised 'past' and a universally applicable "future'." Anthony Giddens, *Modernity and Self-Identity: Self and Society in the Late Modern Age* (Cambridge: Polity, 1991), p. 17.

11 Jon Jerde, quoted in Frances Anderton, *YOU ARE HERE* (London: Phaidon, 1999), p. 198.

12 John Jerde, quoted in ibid., p. 203.

13 Norman Klein, ibid., p. 113.

14 "Dubai Festival City Website Revitalised" (press statement): http://www.dubaifestivalcity.com/press15.html (accessed March 2003).

15 "Genius Loci" is Christian Norberg-Schulz's expression for architecture's pre-modern and site-specific alliance with culture. See Christian Norberg-Schulz, *Genius Loci* (New York: Rizzoli, 1980).

16 Stars Online at http://www.stars.com/art/101757501715460.htm (accessed April 2, 2003).

17 http://www.afwebadmin.com/futtaimwatches/new/details_press.asp?id=860 (accessed January 15, 2003).

18 "Business Vacation©" is one of Koolhaas's patented concepts. "Glossary" in *Pearl River Delta, Project on the City I* (Cologne: Taschen, 2001), p. 704.

19 "The Greens at Emirates Golf Club," promotional literature, 2002.

20 "Emirates Hills," promotional literature, 2002.

21 Ibid.

22 E.C. Relph, *The Modern Urban Landscape* (Baltimore: Johns Hopkins University Press, 1987).

GARETH DOHERTY

5

TERRAIN MARÉCAGEUX:
DUBAI'S LOPSIDED LANDSCAPE

Urban fragments such as buildings, programs, open spaces, and infrastructure that make up Dubai's landscape are organized by flows of
capital, people, goods, and ambition. Together they comprise Dubai's
architectural anarchy, its unlikely urbanism, its fractured geographies
of urban interventions that look like they want to be, and sometimes
ought to be, elsewhere. Such fragmented yet interrelated fields char-
acterize a landscape, and landscape strategies offer ways for intervention and management in such a terrain. Dubai is an imbalanced
landscape, with its real estate and global positioning offset by short-
comings in environmental, infrastructural, social, and political affairs.
A decidedly landscape approach toward Dubai's urban condition
would help rebalance this lopsided situation.

URBAN LANDSCAPE

Landscape and urbanism are often erroneously considered two extremes. Yet landscape and urbanism are really very similar, as both deal with complex sets of interrelated systems arranged over potentially vast areas at the scale of the view from an airplane (or indeed, satellite).[1] Although the composition of Dubai's landscape has since the 1990s been transformed from a desert into a primarily urban landscape, it is still a landscape. Both landscape and urbanism deal with similar-scaled systems, a landscape approach to urbanism is commonly considered to add but environmental dimension, a "soft" strategy, in contrast to urbanism's "hard" economic, political, and infrastructural focus.

Contemporary understandings of the word landscape suggest more than physical space. It has become commonplace to refer to the political, economic, or social landscape—even to a global landscape. Such uses of the word are appropriate because the practice of landscape encompasses all of these factors and more, and they in turn shape the physical, particular landscape. These horizontal factors ought to be considered when reading landscape and considering how to design and intervene in it.[2]

NATURAL SYSTEMS

In landscape ecology, a field of study that attempts to balance the needs of the natural world with those of human beings, landscapes are recognized as mosaics comprised of patches, linked by corridors, and organized in a matrix. For example, a patchwork of fields and woodlands linked by hedgerows and laneways may be organized in an agricultural landscape. Intervention in one part of such an ecosystem, which is often finely balanced, can bring great change to the rest of the system. Likewise, cities are comprised of buildings and open spaces and programs (patches) linked by roads,

Below: Three satellite images of Dubai, 1973, 1990, and 2006; urbanization is marked in red.
Opposite: Real-estate development and the appearance of green landscape are interrelated.

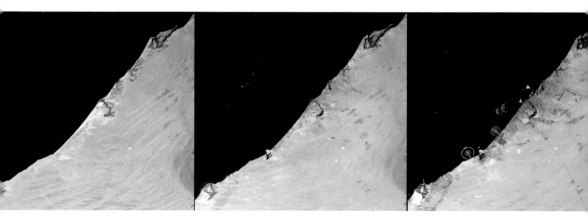

infrastructure, services, and capital (flows) and organized in the urban matrix. Several classifications with similar structures have been proposed for reading urbanism, for example, Kevin Lynch's "paths, edges, districts, nodes, and landmarks," which predate the above classification, and Stan Allen's "points, lines and planes."[3]

Applying such an urban and landscape framework to Dubai, we can see that the city is made up of a series of linked developments such as The Palms, The World, the Arabian Canal, Dubailand, Dubai Port, Jebel Ali Duty Free Zone, Dubai World Central Airport (DWC), the Mall of the Emirates, Ibn Battuta Mall, low-income housing, the suqs, landfill sites, sewage treatment works, and desalination plants, organized within the matrix of global flows of capital and investment, always with the potential of more linkages being made.

Kenneth Frampton reminds us that recognizing the contemporary city—what he calls the megalopolis—as an accumulation of smaller pieces is not a new concept, as cities have historically been formed from an accumulation of parts:

> Cities have always been constructed, in one way or another, out of fragments, and one cannot expect the megalopolis to be any different. Building invariably proceeds by fits and starts. A certain amount of capital is amassed, and when this has been expended, the one-off building process summarily ceases. As architects, we need to conceive of future urban interventions in such a way as they have a wide-ranging catalytic effect for a given amount of investment.[4]

Frampton's point is especially relevant because it foresees an urban development initiated by an accumulation of precise interventions, limited by economic concerns, and intentionally designed to have a catalytic reaction on their surroundings. Keller Easterling stresses that the importance of an architectural project lies in its relationships to other projects around it: "It is possible to understand sites as separate agents that remotely affect each other, that is, the way one can affect point C by affecting points A and B." She suggests that such a flexible approach to city design is an appropriate response to the contemporary network society.[5]

It is not the intervention that should be considered the landscape but the spatial reactions it precipitates. In this sense a building, although primarily a work of architecture, can have significant influence on its surroundings. Take the example of the Dubai World Trade Center (DWTC), built in 1979 by Sheikh Rashid bin Sa'id Al Maktum, father of the current ruler. The DWTC was the first of many mega-developments in Dubai. It was also the precedent for the transformation of Sheikh Zayed Road, Dubai's main artery, now lined with high-rise buildings but as recently as the early 1990s primarily a desert landscape. The DWTC, as the first building in the

But the sand is never far away.

area, needed services such as water, parking, and shops. These infrastructures prompted further development. Construction of the DWTC brought in legions of poorly paid construction workers, mostly from the Indian subcontinent, and they needed accommodation and services. The DWTC building thus had a spillover effect on not just the spatial landscape but the political, economic, and social landscapes of Dubai.

Interventions need not be physical. Dubai's strategic position between Arabia and Iran, its proximity to the Indian subcontinent, and its location vis-à-vis Europe and Australasia have contributed immeasurably toward its prosperity, but free-trade laws were the catalyst that transformed the emirate from a regional trade and (allegedly) piracy hub to a global center for investment and tourism. With the ambitiously named Dubai World Central Airport (DWC) currently under development at Jebel Ali, Dubai will have an airport twelve times the size of London Heathrow, the world's busiest airport.

It is not just Dubai that has developed rapidly with megaprojects; the entire Arabian Peninsula and southern Iran are currently engaged in what adds up to more than $1 trillion in projects. Abu Dhabi, Bahrain, Kuwait, Doha, Muscat, and Kish are all competing to be a "Singapore of the Middle East," a destination for global real estate investment and tourism. Dubai is the prototype for Gulf urbanism, adapting and proliferating interrelated systems over the local and regional landscapes, and what is happening in Dubai is inextricably linked with development elsewhere in the Gulf.

A beach "landscape" looking at the Burj Al Arab.

Landscape historian John Brinckerhoff Jackson reminds us that landscape is not scenery or a political unit but "a system of man-made spaces on the surface of the earth. Whatever its shape or size, it is never simply a natural space, a feature of the natural environment; it is always artificial, always synthetic, always subject to sudden or unpredictable change."[6] Sudden and unpredictable change is the norm in Dubai. Master planning has had little effect despite attempts at controlling and coordinating the growth of the city. The sheer speed of Dubai's development means that it has been changing faster than traditional master planning can accommodate.

Although Frampton calls for a dynamic design, responsive to change, he cautions against the potential open-endedness of such systems in favor of a form of management: "Their 'open' character in this regard should also be capable of being 'closed' when necessary."[7] Frampton calls for a response that is not as fixed as predetermined master plans but not as open as to allow a free-for-all. As anyone will know who has experienced the stagnation of rush-hour traffic, or attempted to cross Sheikh Zayed Road on foot, Dubai is the epitome of open-endedness, where development takes place without sufficient urban infrastructure. Dubai is a response to a mix of market forces and consequently displays the inequalities and imbalances that follow when the full landscape and long-term consequences are not considered in city making.

VISUAL SYSTEMS

Landscape is distinct from urbanism in its combination of the visual with natural systems. The agency of the image distinguishes landscape from urbanism, geography, and planning, which as ways of understanding the earth are primarily concerned with the organizational forces that shape the land. Despite the current focus in landscape discourse on the operational and performative landscape, the etymology of the word landscape, with its origin in the Dutch *landschap* (denoting a picture of natural scenery), reminds us of the importance of the visual in how we use, create, and manage space. The Arabic word for landscape, for instance, *manthar tabi'iyy*, literally translates as "natural scenery"—highlighting that landscape lies in a combination of the natural system with visual constructs. This visual dimension gives landscape the critical advantage over urbanism when it comes to shaping the city.

As can be seen from Dubai's urbanism, the image of a development is critically important for its market success. Through glossy real estate brochures depicting tropical vegetation, green grass, and blue skies, new developments in Dubai, and indeed much of the Gulf, promise triumph over the restrictions imposed by the desert. Projects derive much of their value from the iconic transformative power of changing desert into green, and the haze of sand, heat, and humidity into clear blue skies. Dubai's green spaces are built to sell properties and lifestyles, with the intention of boosting its status as a real-estate investment destination. The image of green is firmly a commodity in Dubai, bought and sold on global markets. The desert is heavily watered daily to construct and conserve the economic value that comes from greenness.

The seductive power of the image is essential to urban development. Often, however, the image is greener than the reality. Many Gulf projects are in the throes of construction, and it remains to be seen how green they will be. If as Orhan Pamuk points out, the primary aim of a landscape artist is to: "awaken in the viewer the same feelings that the landscape evoked in the artist himself," then when the reality turns out not to be so green, the viewer might rightly feel cheated.[8] The idea that something has to look a certain way becomes more important than how it actually looks or works in reality, or the long-term consequences it might have.

LAND ESCAPE

Images lead to dreams that lead to the creation of fractured geographies: places that echo foreign places through their materiality, naming, material form, and color. Through their appeal to global markets, such seemingly implausible projects demonstrate the efficacy of the image of green and its power to shape patterns of urbanization and urban trends and investments, whatever the environmental, social, and political costs. This fractured geography is largely responsible for the sense of fantasy in Dubai's urbanism. Why else are there Wild Wadi Water Parks and ski slopes in the desert?

Images and dreams get built in Dubai. "Welcome to a land that shows the world what can be achieved when you have the courage to dream! A land that offers fertile ground to bring the biggest, most impossible dreams to life!" claims the promotional movie for the 3-billion-square-foot Dubailand, a tourism, real estate, hospitality, entertainment, leisure, and retail megaproject. The DVD begins with an image of the dry, sandy desert being transformed with the help of rain (even though it rarely rains in Dubai), with green grass sprouting and the desert transforming into a forest richly populated with tropical birds and butterflies.

The image of green is a central part of Dubai's urbanism. Aerial views of Dubai show it, like most cities, with a network of buildings and open spaces interspersed with generous patches of greenery. Green spaces such as Wafi Interchange (a large cloverleaf named for the shopping mall to which it leads), Mamzar Park, and the gardens of private family villas are typically carpeted with neatly manicured grass and luscious vegetation. Such green carpets are used to frame views of apartment blocks, hotels, highways, and retail and leisure developments; they signal wealth, progress, and political power.

In 2006, 5.8 percent of Dubai was green, a figure due to rise to 8 percent by 2009 through an ambitious park-building program embarked upon by the Dubai Municipality.[9] Many well-designed and well-intentioned parks have been built in recent years. These parks are typically green and follow Western cultural and aesthetic norms—unsurprising as many of Dubai's new residents bring with them Western ideas of culture and authority. Although parallels are often drawn with the Islamic paradise garden (and in Cairo, "green spaces promote public frenzy"[10]), there is no indigenous tradition of park going in Dubai, locals preferring shaded suqs or air-conditioned shopping malls. Such green urban spaces arguably have a negative environmental impact because they conflict with indigenous ecosystems, disrupting the native desert habitats with foreign and ecologically sterile species. These green spaces also depend heavily on the energy-intensive desalination of seawater.

To meet irrigation requirements, Dubai has become one of the most prolific users of water in the world. Dubai's water comes mainly from two sources: groundwater wells, which have been so seriously depleted through overextraction that treated water has to be pumped back in to replenish the aquifer; and water from desalination plants, which is very expensive to produce. Rough estimates suggest that in the United Arab Emirates, 15 percent of water comes from groundwater recharge; 70 percent from desalination plants; and 15 percent from treatment plants producing water for agriculture and landscaping uses.[11] *The Khaleej Times*, a local English-language daily, reports that in 2002, 181 billion gallons of desalinized water was produced at a cost of 3,426 million UAE dirhams per year, or almost $1 billion.[12] Yet this investment sustains an economy that is built on the notion of realization of the impossible. Scant and irregular rainfall, coupled with a high evaporation rate, exacerbate the water supply problem. To address the issue, the UAE government plans to reuse wastewater to produce recycled water for irrigating green areas; new soil treatment techniques are also being employed. In addition, the private sector is becoming aware of more careful approaches to the water supply. The Palm Jumeirah artificial island, for instance, which had a budget of $55 million for "landscaping," [13] claimed to be incorporating techniques to increase the moisture-retention capacity of the soil, reducing estimated daily irrigation requirements by half, from 15 million to 7.5 million liters.[14] Still, the consequences of imposed greenery are taking their toll, and as the pace of development continues, the situation can only get worse.

Too often there is a tension between what is envirinmentally sound and what the client wants, between environmental good and the image the state wishes to promote. Green has more than an aesthetic and an economic value. It is also politically charged, as the transformative power of green is a potent symbol of progress and of strong, effective leadership. Nelida Fuccaro suggests that the visual references for much of the Gulf's contemporary urban development, including the planting of palms, are associated with the Arab–Islamic tradition and, by extension, such references to an imagined past are a form of political legitimization.[15] Yet the urban trends and expectations that lead to such projects are driven by global markets and taste cultures, ensuring a tension between tradition and modernity in the contemporary Gulf city.

TERRAIN MARÉCAGEUX

When construction was completed in 2006, the Palm Jumeirah had used 110 million cubic meters of sand dredged from the seabed of the Persian Gulf. The island was formed by piling up the sand and supporting it with 7 million tons of locally quarried rock. Such construction is questionable from an environmental point of view and would almost certainly not be permitted if the project were subject to environmental impact statements or the rigor of a Western-style democratic planning process, yet some scholarly articles suggest environmental benefit from such new islands in the form of improved habitats for sea life.[16] Typically islands have been built in the shallowest waters and on top of coral reefs, allowing just one meter for rising sea levels due to global warming. As with their political and social contexts, these are surely unstable ground, a *terrain marécageux*—a French term that relates not just to a physical swamp but also to unstable political and social conditions. The 40,000 construction workers, for instance, who labored on the islands come mostly from Pakistan and India, worked long hours, and were paid low wages with no benefits or prospects for long-term economic or social integration.

The artificial islands are important not just because their construction methods, long-term stability, and environmental consequences are questionable but because they cannot be understood in isolation from the Gulf's nuanced politics, economy, cultural identities, and diverse, complex societies. Designing with and for uncertainty are key features of the practice of contemporary landscape and urbanism, and the extreme

Green landscape needs water.

landscapes of Dubai offer case studies of global urban and landscape trends. Artificial islands and their contexts defy traditional frameworks and professional boundaries. We must begin to understand how they are organized and structured to propose how they might be rebalanced.

Because a landscape is made up of a series of networks, the prototypes must occur at the nodes of the networks, where social, cultural, economic, and political forces meet, a structure not unlike Duchamp's "Mile of String" in diagram. This horizontal network lies not just on the earth's surface but extends over and under it, in what Stan Allen calls the "thick 2D."[17] By affecting certain points on the matrix, a wider landscape change may be prompted than would result from trying to order the whole landscape.

Geographer David Harvey maintains that urbanization consists of a "distinctive mix of spatialized permanences in relation to one another" and that efforts should be directed toward intervening in these processes and their relationships as a way to bring about change, rather than into form per se.[18] Form and image are important, and the client's dream of greenery is the driving force behind many projects in the Gulf. Furthermore, while Easterling's explanation of the networked space is convincing, the links between projects are not so linear, which is why the metaphor of the swampy ground, the *terrain marécageux*, might be more appropriate.

Informal urban developments such as the favelas or slums of Rio de Janeiro are characterized by insufficient physical infrastructures of roads, water, sewage, and drainage; vertical expansion; limited public space; centers for popular capitalism; restricted democratic rights in return for security; and urban form determined by the markets rather than a master plan. Ignoring for a moment the contrast between Dubai's enormous wealth and the poverty of the favelas, the mode of Dubai is not so unlike the structures of these self-organizing slums. Dubai is what TrendWatching.com refers to as an example of "Nations Lite," "a light version of a country or society, like a Diet Coke, stripped of annoying 'features' like crime, bad weather and excessive taxes."[19] This case, where the state provides security and protection from the surrounding desert but not citizenship or such democratic rights as voting, is not unlike the favelas, which offer a bounded environment and protection from within. Just as a landscape approach has been used to improve the quality of life in favelas and make them less environmentally damaging and more socially engaging, a landscape approach can mitigate the effects of Dubai's development.

When in the 1980s it became clear that slum-eradication policies were not working on Rio's favelas, a strategy was adopted to accept and integrate the favelas within their surrounding landscape. Where the favelas met forest, reforestation projects were initiated; when the favelas abutted the city, streets were joined up and given names, and public transportation was introduced. Large-scale flood protection and sewage measures had remedial effects on the wider landscape, not just improving quality of life in the favelas but in the wider city too, by controlling flash floods and pollution. Over time smaller-scale projects began; more recent work consists of "cells" designed to initiate a catalytic effect on their surroundings. An art center in the Jacazerinho favela in the north of the city, for example, becomes a catalyst and a prototype. The most successful projects in Rio de Janeiro's favelas were those that recognized the unique social and building patterns in the favelas and worked with them, rather than against them.

A similar strategy applied to Dubai would help alleviate the lack of coherent thinking and address contradictions in planning and management. A master plan cannot attempt to control the city. Rather, a landscape approach to Dubai would first focus on improving its ecological infrastructure. One sensible approach might cast the desert less as an opposite to green and more as a complement. Reservoirs and sewage treatment plants might be hybridized with leisure facilities, and so forth.

CONCLUSION

Conventional ideas of landscape are not sufficient for understanding the structure of Dubai's urban landscape. A conception of landscape as a visually driven organizational system operating on an urban scale is important if we are to grasp the workings of the contemporary city as in Dubai. Because the image of landscape is part of the problem, such as is the case with urban green, it must also be factored into the solution to the environmental, political, and social imbalances that Dubai presents. A thickened under-standing of landscape becomes necessary, and the very concept of landscape needs to be lifted in the popular imagination, from "soft" areas of leftover green spaces and parks to its actual agency as a primary ordering device for urbanism. [20]

It is not enough anymore to introduce a space, or a structure, or an infrastructure without considering how it will be used and why, and how it may spread over time. Traditional methodologies approach landscape from predetermined criteria such as land-use patterns, transportation infrastructures, settlement patterns, and figure-ground, in a way that neglects the interrelations between the parts and is open to reduc-tive compartmentalization. Landscape analysis needs to address not the physicality of the various infrastructures but their interrelationships and the archetypes that drive them, including visual ideals and images. Land analysis needs to be deeper, higher, and thicker. Analysis needs both *land* and *scape*, both *scenic* and *nature*, thereby leading to new hybrid relationships and more effective use of limited resources such as water and more creative responses to primal instincts such as the desire for urban greenery. The dreams and potentials that drive Dubai need to be acknowledged, not resisted, and link-ages and hybridizations built between the fragments, if the lopsided landscape is to be rebalanced for the long-term good of not just Dubai but the global landscape too.

Notes

Thanks to John Beardsley, Jock Heron, Ahmed Kanna, Moisés Lino e Silva, and Hashim Sarkis for comments on drafts of my chapter.

1   Richard T.T. Forman, *Land Mosaics: The Ecology of Landscapes and Regions* (Cambridge: University of Cambridge Press, 1996).

2   See also Arjun Appadurai, who draws analogies with landscape when he identifies five dimensions of global flow as ethnoscapes, mediascapes, technoscapes, finanscapes, and ideoscapes, in "Disjuncture and Difference in the Global Cultural Economy," *Theory, Culture & Society* 7, nos. 2–3, 1990, pp. 295–310.

3   Indeed, Forman acknowledges Lynch's precedent in *Land Mosaics*, p. 7.

4   Kenneth Frampton, "Toward an Urban Landscape," *Columbia Documents of Architecture and Theory* 4 (New York: Columbia University Press, 1995), pp. 83–93.

5   Keller Easterling, *Organization Space: Landscapes, Highways, and Houses in America* (Cambridge, MA: MIT Press, 1999), p. 2.

6   John Brinckerhoff Jackson, *Discovering the Vernacular Landscape* (New Haven: Yale University Press, 1984), p. 156.

7   Frampton, "Toward an Urban Landscape."

8   Thanks to Enseng Ho, who clarified this point in conversation with the author, March 2007.

9   Orhan Pamuk, *Istanbul: Memories and the City* (New York: Vintage International, 2006), p. 93.

10   Author's notes from a meeting with Dubai Municipality, February 14, 2006.

11   Vincent Battesti, "Cairo Zoo," in Diane Singerman and Paul Amar, eds. *Cairo Cosmopolitan: Politics, Culture and Urban Space in the New Globalized Middle East* (Cairo and New York: American University in Cairo Press, 2006), pp. 489–511.

12   Bana Menon, http://www.geocities.com/Athens/Acropolis/3763/thirst.html (accessed July 15, 2007).

13   Moushumi Das Chaudhury, "UAE Water Consumption One of the Highest in the World," *Khaleej Times*, July 22, 2005. http://www.khaleejtimes.com/DisplayArticle.asp?xfile=data/business/2005/July/business_July470.xml&section=business (accessed July 11, 2007).

14   Calculations are based on information available from http://www.nakheel.ae/Environment/Innovative-solutions/ (accessed July 21, 2007).

15   Nelida Fuccaro, "Visions of the City: Urban Studies on the Gulf," *Middle East Studies Association Bulletin,* Winter 2001, http://fp.arizona.edu/mesassoc/Bulletin/35-2/35-2Fuccaro.htm (accessed July 1, 2007).

16   See F. Al-Jamali, J. Bishop, J. Osment, D. Jones, and L. LeVay, "A Review of the Impacts of Aquaculture and Artificial Waterways Upon Coastal Ecosystems in the Gulf (Arabian/Persian) Including a Case Study Demonstrating How Future Management May Resolve These Impacts," *Aquatic Ecosystem Health & Management* 8 (Jan. 2005), no. 1, pp. 81–94.

17   See Stan Allen, "Mat Urbanism: The Thick 2-D," *Case: Le Corbusier's Venice Hospital and the Mat Building Revival*, Hashim Sarkis, ed. (Munich, Cambridge, MA: Prestel and the Harvard University Graduate School of Design, 2001).

18   David Harvey, *Justice, Nature, and the Geography of Difference* (Cambridge: Blackwell, 1996), pp. 419–420.

19   http://www.trendwatching.com/trends/2003/09/NATIONS-LITE.html (accessed September 23, 2007)

20   See, for example, Charles Waldheim, ed. *Lafayette Park Detroit* (Munich and Cambridge, MA: Prestel and the Harvard University Graduate School of Design, 2004), p. 21.

VIRGINIE PICON-LEFEBVRE

6

DUBAI MANIFESTO: DUBAI'S
RELATIONSHIP TO WATER

Despite abundant criticism of Dubai's architecture and urban design, the city is becoming a successful tourist destination and a model already being exported to other parts of the world.[1] "Dubai is not … yet," states Rodolfo Machado in *Harvard Design Magazine*.[2] Perhaps, but whatever Dubai is today, it is as fascinating as was Las Vegas in the 1970s. What can we learn from Dubai? To follow the path traced by Robert Venturi and Denise Scott Brown, we can probably learn about popular taste in architecture, the invention of a lifestyle, and water management in desert locations.[3] The question of water is especially important politically as well as geographically, as water is becoming a scarce resource and a source of geopolitical conflict. Water management, on the other hand, has to be related to urban models as well as to lifestyles. More specifically, water in its different forms engages all of our senses, our bodies in all of their dimensions, and this is, after all, ultimately the subject of architecture as well.

The position of Dubai in relation to water is especially interesting because the city is located by the desert, surrounded by dunes on one side and the Arabian Gulf on the other. As discussed elsewhere in this volume, the city has planned to build artificial islands in the shape of palm fronds and of the world itself. Images of these projects circulate worldwide and help to market the city as both a new dream destination for tourists and a desirable second home for the rich and famous. The fact that the Palm Islands were on both geographic and media maps even before they were constructed is even more surprising. I was disconcerted to see that only one palm frond was realized, and not even finished, when I visited Dubai in January 2006, whereas the Palm Islands in their entirety were visible on the aerial view shown in my guidebook. This aerial view was, of course, done with a computer graphics program.

In Dubai the real and the fake are intriguingly interlinked. Real dunes and fake islands, real blue sea and fake snow. Even the velvet night sky seems to be an orientalist fantasy. Umberto Eco once wondered why tourists, especially in the United States, preferred the fake to the real.[4] He suggests that the fake is always better than the real because it does not have any defects. The fake Venus de Milo with arms is, in this view, better than the real one. Discussion surrounding the reconstruction and conservation of historic sites is also perhaps related to the question of fakes or pastiche in architecture. As I looked more closely at the relationship of Dubai to water, however, I was able to find different types of relations, carefully designed and defined—more, in fact, than one can see in most cities located along shores. This relation was historically functional before being designed as a way to enjoy the view and to transform the shore into a playground.

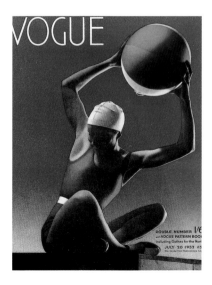

Page 74: One can cross the Creek for a few cents and feel the dynamism of the area while experiencing a new perspective on the city from the water.

Vogue Magazine, 1932

Dubai is currently producing a new form of urbanity, a fragmented urban fabric, and possibly a new way of life not only for the wealthy of Europe and the Middle East, but also for poor workers from India, Iran, and the Philippines, among other countries. The city may therefore be described as a collage of different places: resorts and hotels, malls and commercial developments, theme parks, infrastructures such as the airport and highways, canals and lakes—all of which are juxtaposed in a topographical order. Not everything is perfectly designed, but, whatever the design, it is always intriguing. There is a dynamic that may be compared to the one that Rem Koolhaas described for Manhattan.[5] One can say, at least, that because of its geography, Dubai, like Manhattan, is readable. The line of the shore gives the order of the development, which occurs between streets and highways, built parallel or perpendicular. The desert, likewise, defines a clear limit. The ability of the shore to be a natural and clear boundary is threatened by the plethora of new islands and inland lakes. The shore in Dubai is potentially infinitely multiplied with the construction of artificial islands. At the same time, new residential gated zones are created in the desert around artificial lakes and rivers.

This chapter will develop two ideas. The first is that this passion—or obsession even—to relate water to architecture may be seen in most port and seaside cities (even though Dubai is, admittedly, taking this idea to an extreme). The second is that the multitude of relationships with the water generates a new lifestyle, one based on the assumption that there is no longer a difference between vacation and work. This lifestyle could potentially redefine relations between men and women in a Muslim society, where genders are traditionally separated, as well as become a common ground for the different classes of society; even low-paid expatriates have access to numerous public beaches.

As Margaret Crawford has suggested in a special issue of *Harvard Design Magazine* entitled "Urban Design Now," "the public" does not exist; rather, one should speak about different publics. Since its invention, the beach has been a contested public space, often defined and appropriated by the elite who saw it as their duty to teach the poor and less educated how to behave.[6]

Dubai is designing the set of this water-focused lifestyle. Water, in all shapes and forms, visible and invisible, from the seaside to swimming pools, fountains, and spas, both private and public, becomes synonymous with pleasure, beauty, and endless summer in both traditional and postindustrial cultures. Inside or out, natural or artificial, water is both Dubai's strength and its paradox. It is a paradox not only because Dubai is located near the desert but also because of issues of sustainability.

Contrary to the assumption that everything is gated and privatized in Dubai, the design of the shore offers real and unique public spaces. Public beaches, beach parks, and the urban port each deserve closer study. But before describing such phenomena, I will turn briefly to the history of the invention of the seaside resort to trace the possible origins of some of Dubai's spatial characteristics. Dubai itself invites us to do so. In January 2006, I saw an exhibition for a commercial event in a Dubai mall advertised with a reproduction of an old poster of Nice, a resort that was itself invented (by the British in the nineteenth century) as a winter destination.

قمة متعة الحياة، أبحروا سبعة أيام على ظهر
يخت وأسبوع في جزر سيشل، سيارة BMW X5
ومجوهرات من داماس بآلاف الدراهم!

WHEN SEASIDE RESORTS WERE A MEDICAL PRESCRIPTION

According to French historian Alain Corbin, before Nice became a fashionable destination, the seashore was a place for fishermen and sailors. It was not a place for leisure.[7] The seaside in Europe was generally seen as dangerous, synonymous with death. The ocean was occasionally a site for warfare. Beaches, like cliffs, were places for workers. Nobody knew how to swim, and traveling by ship was always a bit hazardous.

At the end of the eighteenth century, seaside towns began to be developed as winter resorts, and in the nineteenth century, as summer resorts. Doctors played an important role in the invention of the passion for water. They wrote books on the benefits of drinking seawater and they argued that air from the seashore could heal diseases such as tuberculosis and the dreaded nymphomania. Physicians joined forces with developers to lure the leisure class away from another type of water, the spring. Spa towns were the first to capitalize on their situation near bodies of water to attract tourists. These were also the first to use worldwide advertisements touting the benefits of water, a practice that Dubai is now copying to draw visitors.[8]

During the nineteenth century, two types of city coexisted along the shore: harbors grew along a rational pattern to follow the expansion of commercial exchange, and became specialized in the traffic of goods; tourist resorts, such as Cabourg on the Normandy coast, became desirable destinations for the aristocracy. As the industrial city was denounced for its terrible living conditions, the seaside became an attractive destination for the wealthy few who could afford vacations. At the same time, port cities turned their backs on their commercial ports, seeing them as noisy and dirty.

During this period the sea and the coast were still synonymous with fear, if slowly earning a reputation as a venue for regaining physical strength. Being frightened and simultaneously reassured was among the paradoxical experiences of resort developments. As Dominique Rouillard has argued in her seminal study of nineteenth-century seaside resorts, the urban design of such resorts had to provide excitement, perhaps even fear, while remaining safe. One of the most important infrastructures was a sea wall, which functioned both to protect the city and to provide a place for a long promenade along the shore. This promenade was important in the eyes of doctors as a means to promote physical activity, and it was the most desirable location for facilities such as the Casino and the Grand Hotel.[9] The promenade was also the place where people went to admire the sea as well as to be seen, as in Nice along the famous Promenade des Anglais, which was such a public success that it was continuously expanded until it reached the airport, becoming one of the major features of the city.[10] Dubai is following the same track, providing a safe harbor and an exciting waterpark, Caribbean-like beaches and Venice-like canals, as well as wild fishing expeditions in the Gulf and safaris in the desert. The romance of experiencing the sublimity of nature (sea-sky-sand) is advertised worldwide, along with the extreme comfort of Dubai's hotels and residences.

Opposite: A poster from Dubai's Mercato Mall suggests the continuity between Nice and Dubai, with an echo of Nice's Promenade des Anglais.

Houlgate, a typical European summer resort of the nineteenth century

Master plan of Vichy, the model spa town sponsored by Napoleon III

WALKING ON THE WATER

Dubai's fame as a tourist destination derives from images of the Palm Islands and The World project posted in airports and printed in glossy magazines.[11] (The romantic idea that one could own a private island inspired actor Marlon Brando, who isolated himself from the world on a tiny Pacific island he purchased). One may dream of living like a Robinson Crusoe, surrounded by water. In Dubai's case, however, this is a comfortable fantasy, as such islands are conveniently located near the shore, surrounded with stores, hotels, resorts, and restaurants. In addition, the central part of each palm frond is connected directly to the shore with a bridge. If Umberto Eco is correct, a fake island is much more interesting, and probably more picturesque, than a real one. It is, at least, easier to live on.

The experience of Dubai's islands is a fantasy, just as walking along a pier in Blackpool or Nice must have been a fantasy. Among the other infrastructures invented in the nineteenth century for tourists, one must not forget piers. They were at first simple jetties, their original purpose being to cater to the needs of passenger boats, which after the invention of these jetties did not need to rely on rowboats to reach the shore.

Piers appeared with the railroad in the 1880s to attract visitors to new resorts. Such infrastructures originated in England and spread everywhere. They were multipurpose amenities providing diversion for as many as 2,000 people, with kiosks for music, cafés, restaurants, and stores. They sometimes displayed curiosities such as skeletons of giant whales, or included amusements such as casinos or roller coasters. One had to pay to gain access to the platform, which was both an amusement park and a physical experience that gave one the impression of being in the middle of the sea without sailing. Piers also offered a new point of view onto the shore. One can compare the view of Dubai from the Palm Islands to a renewed version of the British piers experience.[12]

Dubai not only provides picturesque beaches, it is also building connections between city and water. Claude Prelorenzo, a French sociologist, has argued convincingly that the Modern movement's ideal city was *green*, whereas for the postindustrial society it has to be *blue*, positioned along the water under a permanently sunny sky. This is also why in 2004 the mayor of Paris organized the *Paris-Plage* (Paris-Beach) to attract Parisians and tourists by transforming the city into a fake seaside resort during the summer. To live near the water and with a view is a common desire for inhabitants of cities as different as London, Montreal, Amsterdam, Boston, New York, and Rio de Janeiro.

It is necessary to explore the reasons for giving water such a prominent role. First, the sea stands as one of the last wild and natural spaces. In many cultures, water is synonymous with life and birth. The presence of water in design is not new. For example, water in Arab gardens such as the Alhambra in Grenada is as important as vegetation. Water changes in meaning after the transformation of commercial ports into urban places. There is often a contradiction between the rational character of quays, for example, and the desire for wilderness.

At least four types of relation with the water are proposed in Dubai: the picturesque (fantasy islands and canals); the historical, as can be seen with the Creek, which
is really a natural port; the contemporary, as seen in beaches such as Jumeira and al-
Mamzar park; and, finally, an urban port type of relation. These different relationships
function like a unique infrastructure, over and under the ground, which generates a
large and irregular grid where residential and office development takes place. The management of water is especially difficult in Dubai, as most of its water comes from the
sea onto sandy ground.

THE SIGNIFICANCE OF THE CREEK AND ITS RELATION
TO SIMILAR PROMINENT FORMS

The Creek is central to the history of the city. Dubai began as a commercial port. The
Creek was the town's first source of wealth, providing a natural shelter for commerce
and smuggling, and it was why the British colonized it and maintained their presence
until 1971. However, since the 1970s the Creek has changed completely. At first it was
enlarged to stop silting, and a new commercial port was built on the shore. The creation
of two banks allowed broad access to water. One side features a long and somewhat
narrow promenade, and the other side a port for light commercial ships called *dhows*.
In its central part, which is the densest, the Creek is a fascinating environment.

A kind of modern Venice, it is here that one sees *abras* (passenger ferries) crossing the water, motorboats speeding to the sea, and *dhows* coming back from Iran or
Pakistan or India laden with tons of eclectic goods, from kitchen oil to hospital furni-
ture. The view from both sides is lively; the commercial activity generates perpetual
movement. The Creek looks like a large open-air corridor buzzing with activity. The
buildings, however, are not as interesting, and none can compete with the Venetian Ca
D'Oro. But from an urban design point of view, they are aligned and collectively define a
consistent and regular façade.

I was interested in the systematic character and simplicity of the different devices
and public facilities that provide shadow, shelter, benches, and toilets. The whole is
remarkable, from the lighting system to the *abra* waiting station. However, this zone
seems to be undervalued by tourists and probably by the Imaratis themselves, because
most of the users are foreign workers, mostly men, who occupy the Creek-side space to
work as well as rest.

Further from the sea, not far from the airport, the Creek looks like a river. Its quality as an urban center is then lost. Past the highway bridge, the Creek's banks are no
longer open to the public and are used as a private marina for the Dubai golf club.
Inland, the Creek transforms itself into a large protected wetland.

THE BEACH AS A SOCIAL MELTING POT

On the Jumeira side of the Creek, on the left bank, past the enclave created by the commercial port, the city stretches along the shore. The urban fabric here is largely the result of subdivisions of villas. This system ends near the Burj al-Arab tower and the Jumeira Beach Hotel. The beach is a simple stretch of sand with many small public facilities, electric lights, and street access along its length. Private beaches are interspersed with public ones. Along the first part of the shore, a large promenade was built for bicyclists, runners, and strollers. There are, however, few cafés or restaurants, and the character is mostly residential. All sorts of people—men and women, locals, expatriates, and tourists—occupy the beach. At the end of the grid stands the Jumeira Beach Hotel by W.S. Atkins and Partners architects, which could have been inspired by Marina-Baie des Anges, a major residential complex near Nice designed by Andre Minangoy and realized in the 1970s by a private developer.

The shape of the hotel, which takes the form of a wave, as well as the elevated, curved structure of the building—features meant to maximize the view for every apartment—are especially reminiscent of Minangoy's Nice project. It is interesting to compare Marina and the Jumeira Beach Hotel because in both cases, the hotel produces a new landscape, a vertical line confronting the horizontal line of the sea, obstructing the view of those located behind the building.

Postcard of Jumeirah Beach Hotel, advertising the landmark with a vivid, attractive image

Facing the Jumeirah Beach Hotel, the Burj al-Arab hotel stands on its artificial island connected to the shore by a 400-meter private bridge. The Burj al-Arab's distance from the coast and the fact that the bridge is designed for car access give the tower a strange position that could be compared to that of a giant lighthouse, playing the role of a landmark. The main argument here, as in the case of Marina, is to maximize the view of the sea and from the sea.[13] Also, in both cases, the landmark building ends the beach like a giant punctuation mark.

THE BEACH AS A LIFESTYLE

It is probably both Rio and Los Angeles that have most developed the beach as a lifestyle. From there, such concepts as fashion, body image, and body language were exported. The beaches in Dubai play an important role in the concept of the leisure lifestyle that the city offers to its more than 1 million inhabitants. In this matter it is important to specify that there are at least four different types of public in Dubai. The least numerous are the Imaratis, who represent less than 10 percent of the population. More numerically significant are the expatriates, mostly workers or merchants from the Middle East and South and Southeast Asia (and increasingly from Africa, China, and the states of the former Soviet Union). These are often called "guest workers" to distinguish them from European, North American, Australian, and white South African expatriates, who are all sometimes called "European." The fourth type is the tourist. The social geography is clear. Near the Creek live mostly the non-European expatriates, while the "Europeans" and Imaratis tend to live near Jumeira. Tourists are everywhere, but some hotels accommodate mostly Russians.

One of the problems that beaches have posed for designers since their adoption as public spaces is their lack of visible or enforceable social barriers. At first, in Normandy, beaches for men were separated from those for women, but it was still difficult to prevent access by undesirables. For this reason, the beach became a model for interaction between different publics. This can also be seen in the context of Dubai, where the public spaces offered by the beach seem to be occupied by everybody.

On the right bank of the Creek, otherwise known as the Deira side, one can find al-Mamzar Park, which provides beaches shaded by palm trees. Users have access to free parking, restaurants, public facilities, cafés, and shaded barbecue areas. One can use the beach until 11 p.m. and swim at night under electric lights. At al-Mamzar, men and women of all nationalities, clad in swimsuits, seem to mingle freely, though there are not a lot of Imaratis. The ambiance is quiet, evocative of a sunny paradise along the ocean. Is it an illusion?

THE URBAN WATER'S EDGE

The Dubai Marina is a large development of residential and office towers, very densely built. The model is no longer a seaside resort, but what I will call an urban port. In the past thirty years, one can identify three different models of urban port. The first is Boston, which transformed its old port into a center for leisure and tourism in order to change its image and encourage the development of existing facilities. Despite the city's declaration to the contrary, the sea edge is confiscated for the (happy) few who have an apartment with a view. The second model is the London Docklands, characterized by the privatization of most of the banks for office or housing developments. The view to the water in these two cases was the main argument to attract developers. In London, the gray water of the Thames is transformed into a metaphor of the blue ocean, which plays the renewed role of the front-yard garden. The third type is Bilbao's proposal, where the water links different public spaces. Which model is being applied to Dubai? The answer is unclear, though it seems that in this matter as in other domains, different elements are appropriated and pieced together.

Dubai is obviously capitalizing on the heritage of leisure-oriented seashores as well as on more recent designs to transform obsolete ports into modern urban places. To become a hub for commerce and finance for the Middle East, the city is transforming itself into a place for tourists as well as business travelers and investors. It is, accordingly, importing and testing every viable model to satisfy every taste: a sort of fusion-architecture and urban design. In Dubai, fantasy, fun, and leisure developments do not target only tourists.

Al Mamzar Park

A Chinese villa at Trouville. Eclecticism signified leisure and an escape from the everyday.

COLLAGE CITY

As a conclusion, one may reference Khaled Asfour, who in a paper entitled "Cutural Crisis" published in the *Architectural Review* denounced what he called the cut-and-paste mentality.[14] One is tempted, after looking at Dubai, to concur with Asfour. But upon closer inspection and with some historical context, one can make the same criticism of the architecture and urban design of most spas and seaside resorts built during the nineteenth-century boom in Europe. The European taste for eclecticism at that time was not so different from the desire expressed in Dubai to paste an Italian-themed mall (the Mercato) near an Arabian-themed hotel (the Burj al-Arab). The difference is the distance between the elements, which is related to the use of the air-conditioned car in Dubai, whereas in Nice or Vichy the urban grid was dimensioned for pedestrians. In these examples from the past, the mélange of styles is amazing. Between the Russian onion dome, the portico from the Italian Renaissance, and a classical French building, one could have seen a neo-Moorish villa and possibly also a Chinese kiosk.

Also, the Promenade des Anglais was cut and pasted into other cities, such as Buenos Aires with its pedestrian promenade along the water, designed by J. N. Forestier. To a certain extent, a summer resort such as Nice may appear as an anticipation of what is happening now in Dubai. The question for Dubai is how to cope with the new context of global warming, pollution, a rapidly decreasing supply of water, and huge traffic jams. It is time as well to reconsider the British-inspired fascination for surrealistic green golf courses. There is obviously not enough rain in Dubai to support this model. It is time to realize that the ideal city has already shifted from *green* to *blue,* or it risks becoming quite brown very soon.

Notes

I would like to thank Hashim Sarkis, who suggested a lecture about Dubai for my class "Cities and Tourism"; Rodolfo Machado, then chair of the Department of Urban Planning and Design at the GSD, who invited me to lecture on Dubai for his studio; Ahmed Kanna, who invited me to the GSD Aga Khan Dubai Workshop in March 2006; the Aga Khan program at the GSD, which sponsored this research; and Saud Sharaf, my student from MIT, with whom I visited Dubai in January 2006.

1   Dubai received about 2.5 million visitors in 2001.

2   Rodolfo Machado, 'Dubai...is not yet.' *Harvard Design Magazine,* Fall 2006–Winter 2007, p. 97.

3   Robert Venturi, Denise Scott Brown, and Steven Izenour, *Learning from Las Vegas* (Cambridge, MA: MIT Press, 1972).

4   Umberto Eco, *Faith in Fakes: Travels in Hyperreality* (London: Minerva, 1986).

5   Rem Koolhaas, *Delirious New York: A Retroactive Manifesto for Manhattan* (New York: Oxford University Press, 1978), pp. 29–79.

6   Margaret Crawford, about Michael Sorkin's essay, in *Harvard Design Magazine,* Fall 2006–Winter 2007, p. 24.

7   Alain Corbin, *The Lure of the Sea: The Discovery of the Seaside in the Western World* (Cambridge: Polity Press, 1994).

8   Anthony Dale, *Fashionable Brighton 1820–1860,* first published by *Country Life Limited,* 1947.

9   Dominique Rouillard, *Le site balnéaire* (Bruxelles: Mardaga, 1984).

10   Claude Prelorenzo, *Nice, une histoire urbain* (Paris: Hartmann, 1999).

11   I saw such a picture in Heathrow Airport during Summer 2003.

12   S. Adamson, *Seaside Piers* (London: Anchor, 1977), pp. 23–43. See also K. Lindley, *Seaside Architecture* (London: Hugh Evelyn, 1973), pp. 33–55; and C. Bainbridge, *Pavilions on the Sea: A History of the Seaside Pleasure Pier* (London: Robert Hall, 1986), pp. 109–143.

13   See, for example, Neil Levine, "Questioning the View: Seaside's Critique of the Gaze of Modern Architecture," in D. Mohney and K. Easterling, eds., *Seaside: Making a Town in America* (Princeton: Princeton Architectural Press, 1991), pp. 241–255.

14   Khaled Asfour, "Cultural Crisis: Analysis of the Arab World's Practice of Borrowing Architectural Designs from Other Cultures," *Architectural Review* 203, no. 1213, March 1998, pp. 50–51.

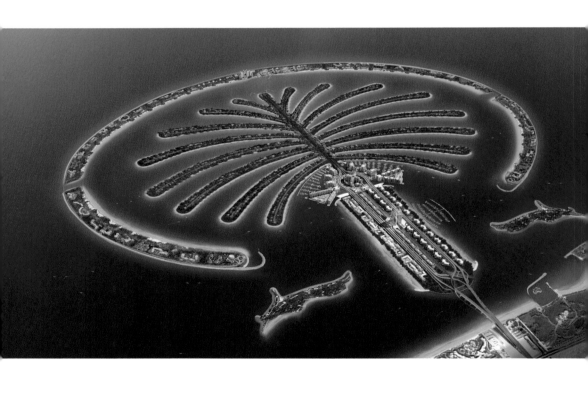

NEYRAN TURAN

7

THE DUBAI EFFECT ARCHIPELAGO

As architecture and urbanism were busy mapping emergent phenomena, Dubai caught us at a bizarre moment. During the last decade, the contemporary city began to be seen as the physical and symbolic manifestation of globalization, rapid urbanization, infrastructures, and networks; research and mapping became more urgent for architecture and urbanism. The terminologies employed by disciplinary frameworks were deemed insufficient when it came to naming and interpreting new urban mutations; accordingly, research on the contemporary city has mapped and documented the immediate and ungraspable evidence of urban conditions as they emerged, at times thickened with a wealth of "retroactive manifestos" that cannot cope with the abundance of evidence.[1]

In this context, as one of the fastest-growing cities in the world and the source of relevant material for such retroactive mapping projects, Dubai is obviously unusual. Busy with prompting unusual templates of scale, Dubai's seductive realities portray the limitations of existing disciplinary positionings regarding the idea of dimension in architecture and urbanism.

In the following text, part of a larger study on the new scales of context within contemporary cities, I examine how Dubai acts as a switchpoint for current discussions on scale. To do this, I try to highlight Dubai's swift mutation not from its locality but from its effects. I propose the idea of the "Dubai Effect," by which I mean the application of the Dubai model of development to other countries, by way of large-scale global projects initiated by Dubai companies. The Dubai Effect is positioned in the essay as an emerging template of large-scale development delineating an awkward symbiosis between the organizational (network) and the iconographic realms of contemporary urbanism. With its peculiar urban and transnational reconfiguration, this symbiosis not only extends our seemingly settled templates regarding the notions of global versus local (as well as generic versus specific) but also asks for new disciplinary frameworks within urban discussions, ones that are reactive and proactive rather than merely retroactive.

THE DUBAI EFFECT

By reorienting the oil-reliant economy to services and tourism (taking Hong Kong and Singapore as its model), Dubai has become the high-speed version of a regional financial hub. To compete at this level, contemporary cities invest heavily in the rapid development of their transportation infrastructures, regulatory and legal systems, and technologies, and aim to provide appealing living conditions for expatriate bankers and the emerging middle classes. In this context, Dubai is the high-speed version of a global city and is becoming a model not only for other cities in the region (such as the financial centers of Bahrain and Qatar, and the Ras Al Khaimah Financial City) but also an important template for more dispersed locations such as São Paulo, Johannesburg, and Istanbul, which are now seeking to become regional financial centers like Dubai. For Dubai, to become such a hub has meant rapid urbanization plus the development of a unique urban form, based on a new port city model.[2] This new model is different both because of its unusual metropolitan organization, land-use systems (i.e., "cities-within-cities," free-trade-zone clusters) and its regulations (such as the independent legal, regulatory, and judicial regime of the Dubai International Financial Center, which may even supersede various federal and/or local laws), and also because of the new templates and configurations it presents at a global scale.

If we map this new model of Dubai not so much from its unusual urban form but through the form of its global effects—that is, urban development projects undertaken by Dubai companies abroad—we see Dubai replicating itself at a new scale and within a new geography. Development and investment projects are packaged and tested first as a brand within their own locality (Dubai) and then exported and franchised adaptively as templates of compact urban organization to various spots in the world. By the

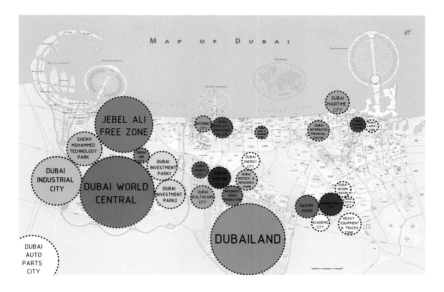

Archipelago urbanism of Dubai

"Dubai Effect," I refer to the global diffusion of Dubai-originated development projects and their potential interaction with these localities. Coupling logistics and infrastructure with tourism and real estate, the Dubai Effect connotes both a literal Dubai authorship and a model for urban development.[3]

The Dubai Effect takes its name from the so-called Bilbao Effect—the self-referential landmark franchising itself for urban regeneration and regional development.[4] With the Bilbao Effect, the building becomes a flagship of seduction for tourism, entertainment, and large-scale urban development projects, which are the "mechanisms...through which globalization becomes urbanized."[5] In parallel, the Bilbao Effect signifies architecture's desire for an alternative reality. Joan Ockman describes the process:

The concept of indigenization affords a more nuanced understanding of the way architectural ideas get disseminated and the experience of their varied materializations. It reminds us that the "context" of any built work encompasses not just the "authentic," pre-existing characteristics of a place. Architecture also has the capacity to embody the often conflicted feeling a place harbors about its own past and future, its insecurities about being provincial, its fantasies and desires for a reality that is alternative to the present. The assimilation of foreign tendencies within a local situation is in this sense not just or not necessarily, a hegemonic process, but sometimes, as at Bilbao, one of voluntary adaptation and a consciously acknowledged need for change.[6]

If the Bilbao Effect marks an aspiration for an alternative reality for a city or region, the Dubai Effect is its expanded and supersized version. That is, if the Bilbao Effect franchises architectural spectacles to promote a desire for change where the flagship building is an icon, the Dubai Effect franchises compact urban packages to encourage alternative futures and the urban model acts as the icon.

Projects of the largest trade infrastructure, real-estate, and investment companies of Dubai—JAFZA, TECOM, Dubai World, Emaar Properties, Damac Properties, Sama Dubai, Istithmar, Nakheel, Limitless—are now spread all over the world, appearing in places as diverse as Saudi Arabia, Bahrain, Oman, Syria, Jordan, Lebanon, Qatar, and Turkey; reaching out to Russia, Kazakhstan, China, India, Pakistan, Indonesia, Philippines, and Vietnam in Asia; South Africa, Djibouti, Egypt, Morocco, Tunisia, Libya, Algeria, Senegal, and Rwanda, Zanzibar, and Mozambique in Africa; Malta in Europe, and the United States.

Large in both scale and investment, and developed mostly with the active participation of local government agencies in each country, these new projects trigger existing real-estate forces and also instigate urban developments in their localities. Just like its predecessor, the Bilbao Effect, the Dubai Effect aims to act as a giant guarantor for further investment. For instance, for one of the Dubai investments in Turkey (Dubai Towers-Istanbul), which was recently cancelled due to ongoing lawsuits and the global economic downturn Dubai's investments promised to activate the property sector as well as fuel further investments in the area. Mayor of Istanbul declared: "The commitment of these [Dubai] giants to the investment property market in Turkey just proves that there is massive potential in the country and that the time is definitely right for property investors to do their due diligence on Turkey and commit to careful real estate investment projects." [7]

THE DUBAI EFFECT ARCHIPELAGO

In March 2006, Dubai's government enacted a law legalizing foreign ownership of property in designated areas in Dubai.[8] The list of freehold properties included twenty-three areas and forty-five plots in the city, including Dubai World Central (previously Jebel Ali Airport City), Burj Dubai, Dubai Marina, the World Island, the Palm Island projects, and Emirates Hills. In addition to the freehold property areas, free zones of Dubai (Dubai International Financial Center, Dubai Internet City, Dubai Healthcare City, Dubai Knowledge Village, Dubai Media City, Dubai Silicon Oasis, etc.) might also guarantee ownership of freehold land within their boundaries in addition to the 100 percent equity granted in every free zone (elsewhere businesses are required to be 51 percent owned by a UAE national). One example is the Dubai International Financial Center (DIFC) Law (issued in August 2006), which allows foreign companies and individuals to hold freehold ownership of real estate within the DFIC. Since entities operating in the DIFC are subject to an independent legal, regulatory, and judicial regime (which may even supersede various federal and local laws), the DIFC is an oasis; it is one of the autonomous island cities of Dubai's archipelago urbanism. In this context, if free zones and freehold areas of the city present a congested form of an archipelago urbanism, the transnational configuration of the Dubai Effect marks an expanded version of this condition, namely the Dubai Effect Archipelago.

An archipelago would be a general term for various forms of enclosure in cities, indicating a fragmented urban condition where autonomous enclaves or islands (that

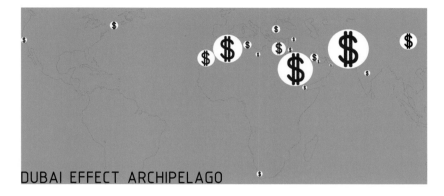

DUBAI EFFECT ARCHIPELAGO

Dubai Effect Archipelago in the global context

is, theme parks, golf clubs, gated communities, special economic zones, office parks, airport cities, IT campuses, retail chains, offshore outsourcing centers, military bases, camps, etc.) are scattered on a common ground. They are "capsular civilizations," as Lieven de Cautier terms them, in elucidating different forms of suburban enclosures in the contemporary city, and spatio-political enclaves or the "critical materialization of digital capitalism," according to Keller Easterling.[9] While the fragmentation of the city is often seen as a twentieth-century phenomenon dating back to the changing nature of the metropolis in the beginning of the century, the fragmented nature of the contemporary archipelago portrays itself as unique—especially with regard to the level of autonomy its islands embody, compared to the vast extent of infrastructural and global networks in which they are embedded. Having different attributes and characteristics and illustrating various forms of what Sven Lutticken calls "parklifes," these islands are paradoxical utopias and zones of detachment, security, extraterritoriality, and exception, where general laws are suspended.[10]

The most important aspect of the Dubai Effect Archipelago is its symbiosis of branding, infrastructure, and real-estate development, providing various combinations of autonomous clusters for different locations. An example of this would be the "SmartCity" joint venture by real-estate firm Sama Dubai and the Technology and Media Free Zone Authority (TECOM)—both divisions of Dubai Holding, owned by Sheikh Mohammed bin Rashid Al Maktoum. Using the autonomous clusters of Dubai Internet City, Dubai Media City, and Dubai Knowledge Village as their model, the aim of the SmartCity venture is to harness the power of existing technology clusters in Dubai and build a large network of knowledge-based industry townships across the world. While exploring the global expansion of various business parks (information and communication technology, media, education, biotechnology, and energy), and coupling those investments with real- estate projects, the joint venture promises technological and economic impact and "sustainable development" to regions. As announced by the CEO of TECOM: "The benefits of the SmartCity concept, as we have seen in Dubai, transcend to all areas of the socio-economic sphere."[11]

In global SmartCity locations, companies will take land on long lease to build their own facilities according to their requirements, just as existing regulations in Dubai allowed construction of Dubai Internet City and Dubai Knowledge Village. In addition to the similarities to existing facilities in Dubai, the SmartCity brand has other features that would be specific to the Dubai Effect Archipelago. For instance, for each company that chooses to be located in a SmartCity in a particular country or region, opportunities is offered to that company to expand into new markets or to set up facilities in other SmartCity clusters located in other countries, creating global interconnections. SmartCity locations are chosen according to their potential to become regional knowledge-economy hubs that attracts "knowledge workers," and local governments' commitment to knowledge-based development is considered an important factor for selection.

One of the first projects of the SmartCity brand is the SmartCity@ Ricasoli (Malta) project, approved by the Malta parliament in 2006.[12] The first European outpost for Dubai Internet City and Dubai Media City, SmartCity@ Ricasoli is promoted by the Malta government as an opportunity for radical transformation of the island's economic activity after its inclusion in the EU. The project is expected to generate 5,600 jobs in the region, and the Malta government sees Dubai's investment in SmartCity as an instigator for other Middle Eastern investments in the area.[13]

The second SmartCity project is SmartCity@ Kochi (Kerala, India). Upon signing the bilateral agreement in 2005 to develop SmartCity@ Kochi, Ahmad bin Bayat, Director General of TECOM, declared: "Dubai Internet City has developed considerable expertise in developing business campuses that provide infrastructure and support services for IT companies...This project is also part of Dubai Internet City's global expansion plans where it is seeking to evolve from a regional venture to an internationally diversified organization. Our mission is to become the ICT business campus provider of choice across the world."[14] Yet full authorization was not granted until some time later because of government resistance in Kerala to Dubai's insistence on freehold rights to the land. The implementation of the project has been cleared by the Indian Ministry of Commerce by declaring the entire project site as a Special Economic Zone for the mega IT facility in 2011.[15] Being a Special Economic Zone means acting like a Dubai free- zone cluster—that is, no foreign ownership restrictions will be applied in developing zone infrastructure, residential areas, and recreation centers in the facility.[16] Accordingly, in Dubai Effect Archipelago urbanism, Dubai island cloning is possible not only by implementing the Dubai urban model for various offshore localities but also by creating necessary regulatory conditions that can provide swift adaptability to these regimes.

The Dubai Effect Archipelago is not limited to the cloning of its technology clusters like Dubai Internet City. Taking Dubai's Jebel Ali Port and Free Zone (JAFZA) as a model, the symbiosis of infrastructure, port development, and real estate would be another form of configuration for the exporting of autonomous clusters. For instance, as part of Senegal's development plans for a new administrative city in the north of Dakar, positioning Senegal as a major business hub in West Africa, the government of Senegal and JAFZA (of Dubai World) signed an agreement in 2007 to develop an integrated Special Economic Zone in Dakar. While the Zone will host 1,000 companies

SmartCity advertisement

within a 6.5-million-square-meter area, the project will expanded to be an integrated port of 10,000 hectares that will include tourism and residential and commercial projects, and will be developed by JAFZA 's sister real-estate companies.[17] Important to note here would be the relationship between the generic and the specific in cloning Dubai Effect Archipelago islands. That is, in an attempt to present the "compact port city" configuration in a specific locality, port infrastructures and facilities are always coupled with business, residential, and leisure areas similar to the development of the Jebel Ali Port, its adjacent Jebel Ali Free Trade Zone, and integrated urban development projects. Another feature of a generic model replication would be the aim for multimodal (sea, air, rail, road) connectivity. Similar to the new airport next to the Jebel Ali Port and Free Zone, Dakar Special Economic Zone's proximity to the Blaise Diagne International Airport is seen as a benefit to the project, enhancing the multimodal idea. Other important international free-trade-zone projects of JAFZA International are Djibouti Port and Free Zone, Orangeburg County Port Project in South Carolina (United States), and Subic Bay Freeport in Philippines.

One development project in Africa seems ripe for the possible provision of free zones as part of the Dubai Effect Archipelago. Dubai's involvement in developing Djibouti's oil terminal, port infrastructure, and industrial and commercial free zone stimulated Djibouti's economic growth, helping it develop as a regional hub for the Red Sea and Indian Ocean, and become a business and tourist destination.[18] The port, now managed by DP World, has become one of the fastest-growing container terminals in Africa.

According to Said Omar Moussa, president of Djibouti's International Chamber of Commerce and Industry: "[T]he relationship with Dubai has made our dream of becoming a commercial centre more real...We are no longer looking at Hong Kong and Singapore but at Dubai." Aboubaker Omar Hadi, commercial director of Djibouti port, summarizes the importance of Dubai's role: "Dubai has done in five years what the French did not do (to help Djibouti) during 115 years of colonization. And Dubai is doing it without showing any arrogance. That is the difference."[19]

Underscoring the strategic importance of Djibouti for Dubai, Dubai-based Middle East Development LLC released its plans in 2007 to build a 28-kilometer bridge (six-lane motorway and four-track railway) to link Yemen with Africa via Djibouti.[20] In addition to the bridge project, the company also announced plans for two new cities (Noor City, translated as "City of Light") to be built at either end of the bridge (Djibouti and Yemen), where both cities will be "tax-free metropolises," and free-trade zones, "having their own law, court system and administration."[21] The details for the bridge as well as the new cities were revealed at a press conference in Djibouti in 2008, at which Djibouti's prime minister participated. Along with the presentations on the Djibouti Noor City, a new airport that will serve both cities was mentioned, providing an air-land-sea link for neighboring landlocked African states.

In that vein, future port projects developed by Dubai in Djibouti and Senegal mark an important feature for Dubai's positioning as a port city and its global connection. In recent discussions on ports, cities, and global supply chains, hinterlands (conventionally interpreted as the background land for the port, or the area over which the port draws its majority of business) are interpreted with their logistical and commodity chain characteristics, in addition to their physical or geographical attributes: i.e., macroeconomic hinterland, logistical hinterland, physical hinterland, etc.[22] It is evident in studies of Dubai's Jebel Ali Port that competitiveness and strategic emphasis on global accessibility and transshipment is the main goal for the port development of Dubai (rather than integrated regional development).[23] Accordingly, it could be argued that projects like Djibouti and Senegal help Dubai's port city to expand into a global hinterland, not only physically but also macroeconomically and logistically. Similar to the recently coined neologism of "development by China"—that is, China's continuing infrastructure development projects in Africa (e.g., in Angola) for an exchange of the continent's resources—"development by Dubai" could mark the initial form of an emerging global reconfiguration and scaling in infrastructural development and urbanism.

"FULL-SPECTRUM CITY PROVIDER"

Of all the projects of the Dubai Effect Archipelago, King Abdullah Economic City in Saudi Arabia—a megacity that spreads across 168 million square meters and is located on the 22-mile shoreline of the Red Sea—represents the most prominent example of the Dubai Effect. Promising potential investors access to both regional and global markets by land, air, and sea, the city is divided into six zones: Sea Port (which spreads across 2 million square meters), Financial Island, Education Zone, Residential Area,

Industrial District, and The Resorts (with an eighteen-hole golf course). Dubai-based real estate company Emaar's positioning of the projects adds to our understanding of the Dubai Effect: "King Abdullah Economic City...signals a strategic move of Emaar from being a property developer to a *full-spectrum city provider*."[24]

This idea of the "full-spectrum city provider" marks the ultimate aim of the Dubai Effect Archipelago: to go beyond the provision of Dubai islands abroad and ultimately to provide compact variations of the Dubai Archipelago City, an integrated provision of infrastructure and urban development. If the Bilbao Effect is marked by the icon of the landmark, located at the juncture of the political and the aesthetic, the Dubai Effect is manifested through the icon/model of "the full-spectrum city."

The "full-spectrum" or self-contained city built from scratch brings the idea of the model back into contemporary urban discussions. An example of Dubai's compact urban model is the "Dubai World Central" (DWC—previously Jebel Ali Airport City), a giant airport city (140 square meters, twice the size of Hong Kong, housing a population of 750,000) planned to transform the region into a powerful global hub.[25] Developed adjacent to the recently completed Al Maktoum International Airport, DWC is a compact airport city, or *aerotropolis*, composed of various clusters: Dubai Logistics City, DWC Aviation City, DWC Golf City, DWC Commercial City, DWC Residential City, and Enterprise Park. Similar to other airport cities such as Hong Kong International Airport and the adjacent Sky City or South Korea's Incheon International Airport and connected New Songdo City, in DWC, aviation-related business clusters and integrated residential and commercial developments enclose the airport.[26]

The strategic location of the DWC next to the existing Jebel Ali Sea Port recalls Dubai's similar aims for the ports and urban developments in Djibouti and Senegal: "full-spectrum cities" interjected onto multimodal (sea, air, land) linkages. Accordingly, with DWC and other similar new city projects in the Gulf region (e.g., the Masdar in Abu Dhabi and the RAK Gateway project in Ras Al Khaimah), one wonders if the next step for the Dubai Effect Archipelago would be the franchising of "full-spectrum" (air) port cities to the world.[27] Considering other similar attempts, such as the currently on hold Dongtan eco-city project in Shanghai, the notion of the self-contained "smart city" from scratch poses urgent questions for contemporary urban discussions regarding expanded definitions of context as well as (urban) models. Evidence of the changing nature of the idea of context is an assertion made by the lead designer of SOM, while discussing the firm's projects in the United Arab Emirates for the *New York Times*:

> Like many architects, Mr. Smith is fond of saying that he wants to make buildings responsive to their context. That can be a problem in the Emirates: most of the time, he concedes, there is no context, at least in the form of surrounding buildings, to respond to. As a result he has turned to a larger context. He explains the buildings' architectural features as responses to geography, geology and climate and is consumed by the notion of making super-tall buildings "green."[28]

Along with all these large-scale projects abroad, the social dimension (i.e., "projected citizens" for those new cities) remains a question. If Dubai, with its expatriate majority, exhibits a cultural cosmopolitanism, for the projects developed abroad, multicultural-ism of the planned cities also seems to be taken into account. As part of the Vision 2010 program, Emaar's acquisition of Singapore-based education provider Raffles Campus is a prime example. To provide educational institutions in its development projects in Dubai and abroad, Emaar attempts with this acquisition to solve the complexities of the multi-cultural nature of their projects: "The world is becoming a smaller place, with global citizenship on the rise. The opportunity to live in a different country and culture will allow our students and teachers to develop a global outlook and be better equipped to meet the challenges of the modern world."[29]

Among all the projects, the crucial question seems to be whether the Dubai Effect Archipelago marks a territorial reconfiguration of globalization as it relates to urbanism and development. If "exceptionality" is argued as the main prerequisite for neoliberal urbanization and large-scale development projects by most theorists,[30] by replicating and reconfiguring its clusters and free zones into various "full-spectrum city" models, Dubai is generating "exceptionalities" within a transnational context. With their separate laws and regulations, these "exceptional zones" act as the culmina-tion of a clever symbiosis between the iconographic branding and the infrastructural realm of urban development. As the autonomous character of the Dubai clusters is often discussed as offering flexible land-use regulation, urban form, and legislation in Dubai itself, it should be added that this new model also allows for easy adaptations into new global locales, strategic cooperation with local government agencies around the world, and varied (infrastructural and iconographic) combinations of "full-pack-age" urban development when needed.

THE DUBAI EFFECT: BIG RECONSIDERED

> The amount of building becomes obscene without a blueprint…Each time you ask yourself, do you have the right to do this much work on this scale if you don't have an opinion about what the world should be like? We really feel that. But is there time for a manifesto? I don't know.
> —Rem Koolhaas, "New New City," *New York Times* (June 2008)

What exactly does the Dubai Effect Archipelago suggest for contemporary architec-ture and urbanism? First is architecture's changing relation to the notion of scale. For more than a decade, with an attempt to analyze and understand our complex urban condition and to develop a repertoire of concepts, research and mapping of the con-temporary city have presented an abundance of retroactive manifestos, providing evi-dence of political and technological imagination.[31] However, rather than exaggerated depictions of emergent phenomena, or an ongoing fascination with the large scale, Dubai Effect Archipelago might portray the necessity to develop new frameworks for

BIG

800
750
700
650
600
550
500
450
400
350
300
250
200
150
100
50

Architecture and the BIG: Le Corbusier's *Aquitania* collage, Rem Koolhaas's Manhattan skyscraper, and Burj Khalifa in scalar comparison

the notion of scale that are less about extravagance and seduction, and more about the possibility of an alternative project for architectural urbanism.

Second, the Dubai Effect Archipelago may raise provocations regarding the notion of the model. For contemporary architecture and urbanism, the large scale, or the BIG, has been a notion that has paradoxically oscillated between being a *symptom* (of emergent urban realities, as described above with research and mapping attempts) and a *model* (for new architectural and urban organizations). It is beyond the scope of this essay to historicize this oscillation within twentieth-century architecture and urbanism; however, some arguments about the symptom and the model condition of the BIG might be helpful here.

"Bigness or the Problem of Large" (1994), Rem Koolhaas's renowned manifesto for the large scale, was an important provocation for a possible attitude toward the BIG within contemporary architecture and urbanism. As the idea of Bigness set the latent theory for scale, the skyscraper became both the symptom and the model for inventive and clever maneuvers within emergent urban phenomena.[32] Koolhaas's admiration for the skyscraper, and manifestly of the BIG, resonated with Le Corbusier's fascination for the ocean liner, best expressed in his *Aquitania* collages. Corbusier showed a clear modernist admiration for the large scale and technological achievement of the ship, perhaps best expressed by his words below the *Aquitania* collage in *Towards a New Architecture*: "[O]ur masterly constructors of steamships produce palaces in comparison with which cathedrals are tiny things."[33]

Here it is important to note the common premise of the BIG scale—and the celebration of the ship and the skyscraper—for Corbusier and Koolhaas. The significance of both lies not only in their expansive scale but more important, in their provocation for a suggestive template for possible urban architectures: the ship and the skyscraper as floating islands independent of any context. Corbusian intervention was like a ship, a *floating city*, conceived as a hygienic separation from the existing urban fabric, in opposition to the unsanitary traditional city. In this vertical garden city, buildings would float on nature, and via urban parks, the ground plane would be liberated for public use. In his book *The Radiant City,* a caption below the cross-section of the *Aquitania* makes evident the direct relationship of the ocean-liner to the proposed urban model, whose functions is to be separated (i.e., housing, recreation, transportation, work). Corbusier writes: "Inside this floating city where all ought to be confusion and chaos, everything functions, on the contrary, with amazing discipline. [M]ain services...are all separately located. Why should a city apartment house not attempt to provide us with the same comfort as a ship?"[34]

Koolhaasian intervention, on the other hand, was like a skyscraper, again a floating island/city, conceived as the hedonistic and zipped replication of the metropolitan culture (i.e., the absurdities of the private domain and its unconventional programmatic and social encounters) detached from the urban tissue yet belonged to the larger metropolitan grid infrastructure. If, for Koolhaas, Manhattan was "a dry archipelago of blocks...[where]...each block is now alone like an island, fundamentally on its own,"[35] (as elaborated in his retroactive manifesto for Manhattan, *Delirious New York*) then, beyond a certain scale, architecture would take the inventiveness of the autonomous skyscraper: independence of context, layering in section for self-sufficient programming, and generic form separating itself from function—all of which would inform a new infrastructural urbanism: "Bigness, through its very independence of context, is the one architecture that can survive...[I]t gravitates opportunistically to locations of maximum infrastructural promise."[36] In parallel, with its clear and necessary replacement of the postwar "contextualisms" and its intricate emphasis on scale, various interpretations of infrastructure urbanisms saw design and infrastructure in a symbiotic relationship. Ultimately, infrastructure became the context itself where operative forces and networks that make the city were emphasized and enacted.[37]

However, as elaborated with the *globally floating islands* of the Dubai Effect Archipelago—in which various combinations of existing clustering models are exported within a transnational scale to provide the "full-spectrum city"—infrastructure is not always a contextual ground. That is, the large-scale urban architectures come at the same time or sometimes even before the infrastructure, where infrastructure might result from the extension of the design intervention. Thus, in these conditions, rather than reacting to a predefined context, designers might be bound to redefine and shape their contexts. This condition not only marks the shifting role of infrastructure in design but also puts pressure on the agency of the architect within a much wider contextual scale. In parallel, while aesthetic and political questions come up front, design decisions cannot be simplified to mere architectural fascination with the extravagance of the BIG or reduced to an innocent extension of external realities. If the Bilbao Effect marked the questioning of the iconographic/self-referential landmark and the role of the architect in our contemporary culture, perhaps the Dubai Effect points a deeper shift for the architect. After a decade of mapping emerging phenomena of the city (the horizontal BIG) on one hand and monumental/expressionist iconography (the vertical BIG) on the other, new disciplinary positions toward the large scale are crucial for architecture and urbanism.

Notes

1. Rem Koolhaas begins his retroactive manifesto for Manhattan by writing that the "fatal weakness of the manifestoes is their lack of evidence." See Rem Koolhaas, *Delirious New York: A Retroactive Manifesto for Manhattan* (New York: Oxford University Press, 1978). Also see Rem Koolhaas et al., *Mutations* (Bordeaux: Arc en rêve centre d'architecture, Barcelona: ACTAR, 2000) and Sanford Kwinter, "Politics and Pastoralism," *Assemblage 27* (1995): 25–32.

2. If we map the evolution of the port-city relationships in history, the story is a one that starts with the port and city being composite parts of a whole (one thinks of the ideal port-city depictions in the sixteenth century) to a complete disjunction especially after the 1960s, and back again to a complete integration effort after 1990s. In the context of the contemporary reintegration discussions of the port and the city, the Dubai model offers a unique urban form via the physical proximity of its port, clusters, and free zones. For a history of city-port relationships, see Josef W. Konvitz, *Cities and the Sea: Port City Planning in Early Modern Europe* (Baltimore and London: Johns Hopkins University Press, 1978); Han Meyer, *City and Port: Urban Planning as a Cultural Venture in London, Barcelona, New York, and Rotterdam* (Utrecht: International Books, 1999); for a review of port-city waterfront relationships, see Brian Hoyle, "Global and Local Change on the Port-City Waterfront," *Geographical Review* 90:3 (July 2000): 395–417; for a specific study on the Dubai Jebel Ali Port, see Wouter Jacobs and Peter V. Hall, "What Conditions Supply Chain Strategies of Ports? The Case of Dubai," *GeoJournal* 68 (2007): 327–342.

3. See "The Dubai Model: An Outline of Key Components of the Development Process in Dubai," *Working Paper No. 12* (October 2007), Centre for Contemporary Middle East Studies, University of Southern Denmark, http://www.sdu.dk/~/media/246A1730F5C34E2893FC512BF694E28F.ashx; "Public-Private Ties and Their Contribution to Development: The Case of Dubai," *Middle Eastern Studies* 4:43 (July 2007): 557–577.

4. For discussions on the "Bilbao Effect," see A. M. Guasch and J. Zulaika, eds., *Learning from the Bilbao Guggenheim* (Reno: Center for Basque Studies, 2005); and G. C. Santamaria, *Bilbao: Basque Pathways to Globalization* (Oxford: Elsevier, 2007). To promote Bilbao as a new cultural and business center, the Guggenheim Museum was one of two major landmarks in a waterfront development project that also included the construction of 80,000 square meters of office space, a 27,000-square-meter shopping center, a luxury hotel, university facilities, and 800 housing units, and 122,000 square meters of green space. See Frank Moulaert, Arantxa Rodriguez, and Erik Swyngedouw, "Neoliberal Urbanization in Europe: Large-Scale Urban Development Projects and the New Urban Policy," *Antipode* 3 (July 2002), 542–582. For more on the Bilbao Effect and the relationship between urban development and museums, see C. Hamnett and N. Shoval, "Museums as Flagships of Urban Development," in *Cities and Visitors: Regulating People, Markets, and City Space*, edited by L. M. Hoffman, D. Judd, and S. S. Fainstein (Oxford: Blackwell, 2003), 219–236. Among references to the relationship between the Bilbao Effect, architecture, spectacle, and branding are: D. Medina Lasansky and Brian McLaren, eds., *Architecture and Tourism: Perception, Performance, and Place* (Oxford and New York: Berg, 2004); Joan Ockman and Salomon Frausto, *Architourism: Authentic, Escapist, Exotic, Spectacular* (Prestel, 2005); A. Klingman, *Brandscapes: Architects in the Experience Economy* (Cambridge, MA: MIT Press, 2007); Anthony Vidler, *Architecture Between Spectacle and Use* (Williamstown, MA: Sterling and Francine Clark Institute, 2008).

5. "In sum, large-scale urban development projects are the mechanisms *par excellence* through which globalization becomes urbanized." Frank Moulaert, Arantxa Rodriguez, and Erik Swyngedouw, eds., *The Globalized City: Economic Restructuring and Social Polarization in European Cities* (New York: Oxford University Press, 2003), 3.

6. Joan Ockman, "New Politics of the Spectacle: 'Bilbao' and the Global Imagination," in *Architecture and*

Tourism: Perception, Performance and Place,
edited by D. Medina Lasansky and Brian McLaren
(Oxford, New York: Berg, 2004), 235.

7   "Mayor Topbas: 'This Tender is the Expression of
    Turkey's Stability and Istanbul's Opening-up to
    the World," *Istanbul Municipality News*, March 23,
    2007, < http://www.ibb.gov.tr/IBB/Popup/en-US/
    PrinterFriendlyHaberler.aspx?CultureId=en-
    US&HaberId=1065> (March 25, 2007). In 2007, a large
    tract of public land was sold to Sama Dubai by
    the Turkish Government via a controversial public
    auction that attracted much local criticism and
    lawsuits. Sama Dubai could not pay the necessary
    amounts by 2010 and the land has recently been
    transferred back to the Turkish Government.

8   In 2002, the Ruler of Dubai announced that free-
    hold ownership of certain designated areas within
    Dubai would be available to all nationalities.
    However, no laws or regulations reflecting permit-
    ted foreign ownership of the relevant designated
    areas were enacted in Dubai until 2006.

9   Lieven De Cautier, "The Capsule and the Network:
    Preliminary Notes for a General Theory" *Oase*
    54 (2001): 122–134; Keller Easterling, *Enduring
    Innocence: Global Architecture and Its Political
    Masquerades* (Cambridge, MA: MIT Press, 2005), 1.

10 Sven Lutticken, "Parklife," *New Left Review 10* (July/
    August 2001): 111–118. For an analysis of contem-
    porary island conditions as utopias, see Stephen
    Coates and Alex Stetter, eds., *Impossible Worlds*
    (Basel, Boston: Birkhäuser, 2000); and Anselm
    Franke, Rafi Segal, Eyal Weizman, eds., *Territories:
    Islands, Camps, and Other States of Utopia*
    (Cologne: Verlag der Buchhandlung Konig, 2003).

11 "TECOM and Sama Dubai to Jointly Create 'Smart
    City' Clusters Worldwide," *Sama Dubai News*,
    March 20 2007,<http://www.sama-dubai.com/
    news/070320A.asp> (retrieved on March 27, 2007).
    For details on the project, see: www.smartcity.ae.

12 Smart City@Malta project opened its initial build-
    ings in 2010 and will be fully completed in 2021.

13 For an interview with the prime minister of Malta
    (Lawrence Gonzi) regarding the Smart City@Malta
    project, see: Mohammed Ezz Al Deen, "Malta's
    Dubai-Backed Smart City Will Put Island on IT Map,"
    Gulf News, March 30, 2007, http://archive.gulfnews.
    com/articles/07/03/30/10114645.html (retrieved on
    April 1, 2007).

14 Vimala Vasan , "Kochi Smart City: DIC Plans Study
    for Prospective Firms," *Business Line*, September
    12, 2005, http://www.thehindubusinessline.
    com/2005/09/12/stories/2005091200681300.html
    (retrieved on November 15, 2006). "SmartCity Kochi
    Go-Ahead," *AME Info*, May 13 2007, http://www.
    ameinfo.com/119959.html (retrieved on May 17,
    2007).

15 The Government of India has granted a single
    Special Economic Zone (SEZ) status for the 246
    acres of project land in December 2011. See the
    official announcement at the website of Special
    Economic Zones of India, Ministry of Commerce,

<http://www.sezindia.gov.in> (retrieved on
December 10, 2012). The Smart City@Kochi is
planned to have an 8.8 million square feet of built-
up space.

16 "Tecom's Kerala Smart City Project Gets SEZ
    Status," *Khaleej Times Online*, 21 March 2008, http://
    www.khaleejtimes.com/DisplayArticle.asp?xfile=/
    data/business/2008/March/business_March643.
    xml&section=business (retrieved April 1, 2008).

17 A $709-million contract was already signed by
    JAFZA's sister company, marine terminal operator
    DP World, and the Senegal Government to upgrade
    the Port of Dakar and build a container terminal.
    The contract for the Dakar Special Economic Zone,
    on the other hand, was signed in 2008 by JAFZA to
    develop a free zone of 6.5 million square meters.

18 While JAFZA manages Djibouti Free Zone and Dubai
    Customs, DP World has invested $30 million in the
    Horizon Djibouti Terminal facility and committed
    $300 million for a new container port. In addition to
    infrastructural projects, Nakheel is developing its
    first overseas development, a five-star hotel at the
    center of Djibouti City, the capital of Djibouti. For
    the expansion and redevelopment of the Djibouti
    port, several Arab financial institutions are also
    involved: the Arab Fund for Social and Economic
    Development (AFSED) and funds from Saudi Arabia,
    Kuwait, and Abu Dhabi. Djibouti also houses the
    only American military base (Camp Lamonier, previ-
    ously the military barracks of the French Foreign
    Legion) in Africa since 2001.

19 "Dubai Projects Stimulate Djibouti Economic
    Growth," *Gulf News*, April 1, 2006, http://archive.
    gulfnews.com/articles/06/04/01/10029826.html
    (retrieved September 12, 2006).

20 Danish consulting engineering group COWI has
    been commissioned for the giant project. See
    "Yemen: Africa Bridge," *AME Info*, February 2, 2007
    <http://www.ameinfo.com/111352.html> (March
    5, 2007). See also the project announcement in
    Denmark's Ministry of Foreign Affairs news note:
    "Danish Engineers to Design Giant Bridge over Red
    Sea," March 13 2008 http://www.investindk.com/vis-
    Nyhed.asp?artikelID=19277 (retrieved April 2, 2008).

21 The bridge project is on hold since 2010 mainly
    due to the recent Dubai credit crunch as well as
    the civil uprisings in Yemen. See the earlier article
    in *Economist* about the proposed plans regarding
    Djibouti and Yemen: "The Red Sea: Can It Be Really
    Bridged?" *Economist* (August 2, 2008): 55–57. Also
    see: Horand Knaup, "A Vision to Connect Africa and
    Asia," *Der Spiegel* (August 22, 2008).

22 Theo Notteboom and Jean-Paul Rodrigue,
    "Re-assesing Port-hinterland Relationships in the
    Context of Global Commodity Chains," in *Ports,
    Cities, and Global Supply Chains*, James Wang et al.,
    eds. (London: Ashgate, 2007), 51–66.

23 Jacobs and Hall, "What Conditions Supply Chain
    Strategies of Ports? The Case of Dubai."

24 [italics added]. "Emaar Showcases International
    Projects of over AED 220 Billion at Cityscape,"*INR

News, December 2, 2006, http://www.inrnews.com/realestateproperty/middle_east/dubai/emaar_showcases_international.html (retrieved January 16, 2007).

25 The airport has an annual cargo capacity of 12 million tons, more than three times that of Memphis International Airport, and a passenger capacity of more than 120 million.

26 *Aerotropolis* is a term coined by John Kasarda, professor of management at the University of North Carolina's Business School. Greg Lindsay, "The Rise of the Aerotropolis," *Fast Company* 107 (July/August 2006): 76–85; for a detailed discussion on the topic, see John Kasarda, *Airport Cities: Evolution* (London: Insight Media, 2008).

27 Masdar (which means "the source" in Arabic) Eco-City is a 6-square-kilometer zero-pollution, zero-waste city for 100,000 people, designed by Norman Foster. Construction began on Masdar City in 2008 and the first buildings of the city were completed and occupied in October 2010. Full completion is scheduled for 2025. Masdar City will employ various renewable power sources. Solar power plants, wind farms, geothermal energy, solar power plants, solar-powered desalination, gray-water recycling, waste incineration, and sustainable manufacturing are all planned for the project.

28 Fred. A. Bernstein, "Reaching for the Clouds in Dubai," *New York Times* (August 8, 2008).

29 Raffles Campus, which is registered with the Ministry of Education in Singapore, has six educational institutions in Singapore, Vietnam, Indonesia, and China. See "Emaar Acquires Singapore-Based 'Raffles Campus' to Provide World-class Education," http://www.emaar.com/MediaCenter/PressReleases/2006September26.asp; also see http://www.rafflescampus.com/pressrelease1.asp

30 Especially in terms of urban policy making, exceptionality is argued as the main driving force for large-scale urban development projects: "The framework of 'exceptionality' associated with these initiatives favors a more autonomous, if not autocratic, dynamic marked by special plans and projects that relegate statutory norms and procedures to a secondary and subordinated place… 'Exceptionality' is a fundamental feature of the new urban policy, based on the primacy of project-based initiatives over regulatory plans and procedures." Frank Moulaert et al., "Neoliberal Urbanization in Europe: Large-Scale Urban Development Projects and the New Urban Policy," 577. For an interesting reflection on the idea of exception and its relation to neoliberalism and globalization, see Aihwa Hong, *Neoliberalism as Exception: Mutations in Citizenship and Sovereignty* (Durham and London: Duke University Press, 2006).

31 A typical example of the research/mapping attempts would be the documentation of Rem Koolhaas's *Harvard Project on the City.* See Rem Koolhaas et al., eds., *Great Leap Forward* (2002), *Mutations* (2001), and *Harvard Design School Guide to Shopping* (2002), all published by the Harvard Graduate School of Design. Also see Kazys Varnelis, "Is There Research in Studio?" in *Journal of Architectural Education* 61:1 (2007): 11–14.

32 Rem Koolhaas, "Bigness or the Problem of the Large," *Small, Medium, Large, Extra-Large: Office for Metropolitan Architecture,* edited by Jennifer Sigler (Rotterdam: 010 Publishers; New York: Monacelli Press, 1995), 495–516.

33 The quote as it appears below the *Aquitania* collage: "Architects live and move within the narrow limits of academic requirements and in ignorance of new ways of building, and they are quite willing that their conceptions should remain as doves kissing one another. But our daring and masterly constructors of steamships produce palaces in comparison with which cathedrals are tiny things, and they throw them on to the sea. Architecture is stifled by custom." Le Corbusier, *Towards a New Architecture* (New York: Praeger Publishers, 1970).

34 Le Corbusier, *The Radiant City: Elements of a Doctrine of Urbanism To Be Used as the Basis of Our Machine-Age Civilization* (New York, Orion Press, 1967), 118.

35 Koolhaas, *Delirious New York,* 97.

36 Koolhaas, "Bigness or the Problem of the Large," 515.

37 For some of the early theoretical and practical variations of infrastructural urbanisms, see Alex Wall, "Programming the Urban Surface," *Recovering Landscape,* ed. by James Corner (New York: Princeton Architectural Press, 1999), 232–249; and Stan Allen, "Infrastructural Urbanism," in *Points + Lines* (New York: Princeton Architectural Press, 1999), 46–57. Also see Charles Waldheim, *The Landscape Urbanism Reader* (New York: Princeton Architectural Press, 2006) and Rem Koolhaas, "Urban Operations," *D: Columbia Documents of Architecture and Theory,* vol. 3 (1993): 25–57.

YASSER ELSHESHTAWY

8

RESITUATING THE
DUBAI SPECTACLE

In this chapter, I try to go beyond the aesthetic focus on Dubai. In my research, I look at the city through two perspectives: first, through its impact on the Arab world's more traditional cities, which has turned out to be quite extraordinary; and second, through the prism of what I call the city's forgotten urban public spaces, a topic that in turn raises issues of social exclusion and resistance. By situating the city within its regional and social contexts, we can begin to move away from conventional views. Although I suggest avenues for further research on the second issue, my focus in this chapter will be on the first.

It has become fashionable to read Dubai as a typical city of postmodern illusion and aesthetic excess. Such a view, to paraphrase Jean Baudrillard (describing Los Angeles), would note that the city is nothing more than an immense script and a perpetual motion picture that is, in turn, based on faked phantasm.[1] This reading certainly does apply to some aspects of Dubai. Here the city becomes an amalgamation of unrelated "nodes" connected through a virtual network. This perspective, however, underestimates the influence that is exerted when a city generates a model that is "easily translatable" or exportable. I argue that this is exactly the case of Dubai in its Middle East context.

Traditional Arab cities are recognizing the dominance of emerging centers such as Dubai and are now engaged in a process of catch-up and emulation. This is in many instances instigated by local governments, but also through foreign investment. Gulf countries in particular, flush with money from oil sales, are looking beyond their immediate surroundings and, in an attempt to export their capital, are investing in these traditional centers. The urban streetscape of cities such as Cairo is being transformed, filled with the symbols of global capital, through billboards promising the good life and the placement of luxurious mixed-use developments, albeit in proximity to sub-standard public housing projects. These projects emphasize a lifestyle based on consumerism, such as can be seen in various advertisements. Many people are left behind, however, reduced to passivity and forced to observe the spectacle from a distance.

Page 104: The Madinat Jumeirah project, with the Burj al-Arab in the background
Below: Observing Dubai's aerial image at the Dubai Cityscape 2005 Real Estate Exhibition

Top: Advertisement for the City Center Mall, anchored by the French supermarket chain Carrefour, on a main highway surrounded by middle-class housing projects
Bottom: An advertisement by EMAAR, Dubai's premier real-estate developer, promising a massive expansion in the region

For better or worse, Dubai has become a model for cities both in the Gulf and the broader Arab world, such that phrases like "the Dubai model" and "Dubaization" are entering scholarly discourse. At a more popular level, the word Dubai is synonymous with unabashed consumerism. For example, a popular shopping center in Algiers is called the Dubai market (Suq Dubai).[2] In the process, cultural values are being commodified to cater to the desires of a global capitalist elite, essentially turning the entire city into a giant Debordian spectacle. To understand the notion of influence, I will discuss projects currently under way in the Arab world's traditional centers that are a direct response to, and an emulation of, projects in Dubai. I will conclude by suggesting the possible dangers such projects pose within the context of Middle Eastern urbanism.

THE DUBAI SPECTACLE

Guy Debord, in his widely read polemic "The Society of the Spectacle," offers a damning vision of consumerist society. He notes that in societies where modern modes of consumption prevail, life becomes an "immense accumulation of spectacles." It can come in many forms, such as information, propaganda, and advertisement, and it permeates all types of social relations and perceptions. Debord suggests that the society of the spectacle demands an attitude of "passive acceptance," a passivity that is triggered by the spectacle's "manner of appearing without reply, by its monopoly of appearance." Furthermore:

> The spectacle's externality with respect to the acting subject is demonstrated by the fact that the individual's own gestures are no longer his own, but rather those of someone else who represents them to him. The spectator feels at home nowhere, for the spectacle is everywhere.[3]

Thus the spectacle can contribute to a general sense of alienation by emphasizing the disconnectedness between observers and the material, physical object. While Debord's focus is on the mass media, one can clearly project this to the built environment. This phenomenon becomes particularly evident in a city such as Dubai, which is in essence a tabula rasa "obsessively building itself into significance," according to one observer.[4] The only way it can create this significance is by sheer exaggeration, focusing on superlatives (the tallest, the biggest, etc.) irrespective of any relation to local context. The result is a fragmented, splintered urban fabric. Its widely discussed megaprojects seem to exist in a parallel universe within an endless desertscape.

Debord adopts a Marxist perspective, criticizing contemporary modes of production. He was also a proponent of the Situationist movement, prominent in the 1960s, so his writings are related to a context that is very different from that of a Gulf city-state. Yet it is interesting to note that such a viewpoint is echoed by contemporary Marxist thinkers such as David Harvey and Mike Davis. For example, Davis, in an article for *Mother Jones* titled "Sinister Paradise," argues that something called "urban capitalism" has manifested itself with particular intensity in Dubai.[5] The symbols of urban capitalism are without question the city's mega-developments. I will briefly discuss three projects which typify what I call, following Davis, the "urban spectacle": the Madinat Jumeirah project, the Wafi City shopping and entertainment center, and the Burj Khalifa.

Madinat Jumeirah is an exclusive mixed-use complex located in the upscale Jumeirah district, next to the Burj al-Arab hotel. It contains a hotel, a shopping center, a spa, and a conference center. Of particular interest is the use of an imaginary archetypical Arab cityscape. It is described as the "Arabian Resort of Dubai," a "mag-

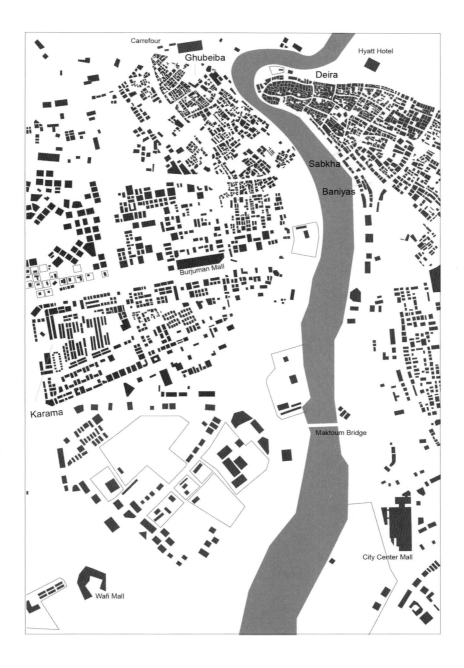

A figure-ground diagram of Dubai's central area

nificent tribute to Dubai's heritage, ... styled to resemble an ancient Arabian citadel."
Furthermore, its "meandering waterways transport guests to all parts of this intricate
city of senses."[6] There are a number of images at work here: Dubai heritage, an Arabian
citadel, and some sort of Venice. The architecture does in fact relate to these images.
In particular, Dubai's ubiquitous Iranian-inspired *barajeel*, or wind towers, are exaggerated in scale so that they become a defining feature of the project's skyline. Here
the project's architects were influenced by the Bastakiyya district, a traditional area
in the heart of the city founded by Persian migrants at the beginning of the twentieth
century, who used the wind tower to promote air circulation. To further this notion of
a new Arabian center, advertisements in business trade publications utilize traditional
imagery, transplanting the hotel into an orientalist painting, an attempt both to claim
the title of the new center of the Middle East and to cater to the fantasies of a global
clientele. Rather than being constrained by any reality, this project initiates a new tradition and heritage by reconfiguring such historic elements.

Using similar tactics but addressing another cultural era is Wafi City shopping and
entertainment center. The project deploys Pharaonic imagery throughout its sprawling
complex; entry points are decorated with Pharaonic statues, hieroglyphs cover surfaces, and so on. A hotel takes the shape of a giant pyramid. Again, historical images are
appropriated and reconfigured to create a spectacle. According to a Dubai Municipality
official, "In 2002, the Egyptians got 5.3 million tourists and we got 4.7 million. They have
the pyramids, and they do nothing with them. Can you imagine what we'd do with the
pyramids?"[7] Apparently, you build your own, which will indeed be done soon, in the
gigantic Dubailand project, a Disneyesque development currently under construction.

Entrance to a spa at the Wafi City complex

The last project, Burj Dubai (now Burj Khalifa), exemplifies perhaps more than any other the notion of the urban spectacle.[8] At over 750 meters, it is meant to be the tallest building on earth, surpassing the current record holder, TAIPEI101, which is 540 meters tall. The design of the Burj Khalifa is based, according to its developer, EMAAR, on a "desert flower." Thus the tower not only "reflects the unique desert light, but the unique culture and environment of Dubai." It is further claimed that the architect, Adrian Smith from Skidmore Owings and Merrill, "incorporated patterns from traditional Islamic architecture. According to official project sources, "He drew inspiration from a flower. The Hymenocallis is a plant that is widely cultivated in Dubai, in India and throughout this region. The flower's harmonious structure is one of the organizing principles in the tower's design."[9] This flower is obviously not unique to Dubai, nor was it a direct inspiration. Rather, these conceptual musings were added after the design was submitted.[10] Of interest is the discourse created around the construction of this tower. For example, its advertisements prominently display a rendered view with the words "History Rising," indicating that the construction of this tower heralded the dawn of a new history for Dubai.

The discourse of modernity plays a prominent role in justifying the construction of such a gigantic building. By deciding to place this tower in Dubai, the city proclaims itself to be truly modern, irrespective of the fact that the building is designed by an American firm, constructed by a Korean construction company, with construction work carried out by Asian laborers, and with most of the apartments and hotels purchased by an expatriate clientele. Despite these global orientations, the developers felt the need to contextualize the project and give it an "Arabian" touch, whether through some imaginary conceptual direction or the creation of pseudo-Arabian districts within

A new history for Dubai

the overall development. Finally, this takes place within a discursive rather than an actual space.

Yet these projects point out a much larger problem that transcends the context of Dubai and the Gulf. As Debord notes, the spectacle can contribute to a general sense of alienation by emphasizing the disconnectedness between observers and the material, physical object. The creation of these fragments within the desert, objects that are inaccessible except by the wealthy, may eventually lead to dissatisfaction and social problems. Furthermore, theming is a common device employed by developers and investors throughout the world, enticing visitors by creating a fantasy environment. Dubai has merely intensified this logic by allowing theming to become a defining character of an entire city to such an extent that a recent *Economist* article on themed parks in the United States is titled "Dubai in America."[11] Thus the word Dubai is becoming synonymous with artificiality. Images such as these are powerful, acquiring lives of their own, according to Debord (who argues that the "globalization of the false is also the falsification of the globe").[12] Falseness becomes a virtue, a model: "What is false creates taste, and reinforces itself by knowingly eliminating any possible reference to the authentic. And what is genuine is *reconstructed* as quickly as possible to resemble the false."[13] In the next section I will describe the impact of the Dubai spectacle on the Arab world and its traditional centers, which in many ways is an affirmation of Debord's predictions.

REGIONAL INFLUENCES: THE DIFFUSION OF THE SPECTACLE OR "DUBAIZATION"

For decades it was the big, central Arab powers that set the tone for the Arab world and led innovation. But today the region is being led from the outer edges. It's the little guys that are doing the most interesting stuff, and it's the big guys that will be left behind if they don't wake up.
—Thomas Friedman, *New York Times*[14]

Until recently, it was a commonplace among both local and international media to show the supremacy of Dubai over other Middle Eastern cities as well as its determination to join the ranks of leading world cities. Outside of such anecdotal evidence, however, does data support Dubai's perceived supremacy and success?

Other than a report commissioned by the United Nations mildly supporting this view, there is unfortunately a paucity of good empirical research that might help in evaluating the glowing reviews of Dubai.[15] Moreover, Dubai's recent economic difficulties have been generating less positive media coverage, at least internationally. But another way to understand the extent of Dubai's influence is to look at the ways in which its major corporations export their urban vision. A good example is EMAAR.[16] EMAAR's projects in Egypt include Cairo Heights, an exclusive $4 billion residential development; Smart Village, an integrated community located next to Cairo's information technology center; and Bibliotheca Alexandriaa, a waterfront development project in Alexandria. The company was also awarded a lucrative development project located on Egypt's Mediterranean coast, an area that encompasses 6 million square meters.

In Morocco, EMAAR's projects include Amelkis II, a $327-million luxury residential golfing complex, and Bahia Bay, a $1.2-billion residential golfing community. Another series of projects are planned, part of a $5.34-billion agreement between the Moroccan government and EMAAR: Oukalmeden, a project for a "four season mountain destination for recreation, entertainment and relaxation, as well as … the Middle East and Africa's only golf and ski resort; Saphira, a development located on Rabat's western side set 'to become the leisure and tourism hub of Rabat city;' " while next to Tangiers, Tinja will be a marina and luxurious seaside development. In Syria, EMAAR is planning the Eighth Gate, a $500-million residential development. The developers of the Eighth Gate note that it is the first gated community in Syria and that it "builds upon the ancient history of Damascus in its architectural style of ornately decorated buildings influenced by traditional Islamic design and (that it) pays homage to the city's ancient roots, … the people of Damascus will soon be able to experience an Eighth Gate, one that retains the best of the past but in a modern context." In Tunisia, EMAAR is developing Marina Al Qussor, a $1.88-billion development on the country's eastern coastline. Its size is 442 hectares, about 4.5 million square meters.[17] Other projects are planned in Saudi Arabia (King Abdullah Economic City) and Sudan as well as in Istanbul (Dubai Tower) and Pakistan.[18]

These projects appropriate regional elements (e.g., the gates of Damascus), apply them to unexpected contexts (e.g., entry to a gated community), and add other stylistic elements (e.g., arches, decorations, etc.), thus reworking the symbolism of the original and creating a new image. This new image, in turn, becomes in itself a point of reference, a Debordian spectacle. The case of Cairo, the traditional center of the Arab world, is a good example of the extent of Dubai's regional influence.[19]

In looking at the directionality of influence in Cairo, two possible areas of investigation exist: 1) state-sponsored projects, which adopt an idea without copying its form in a direct manner; such projects are modeled on similar ventures throughout the world; 2) investment from Dubai-based companies, directly applying a successful Dubai formula.

The first category in Cairo includes the Smart Village project, modeled after Dubai's Internet City; the second category includes the City Center shopping mall concept introduced by Dubai's Al-Futtaim group. Both are Dubai-based ideas, but they are not unique to the city and occur in other centers throughout the world in different forms. Internet City, for example, is modeled after Silicon Valley and technology parks in Southeast Asia. The hypermarket is not a Dubai invention but occurs throughout the developed world. However, the singularity of these projects within an Egyptian context, occurring after their success in Dubai, does suggest a strong influence, particularly with regard to the City Center project. How do these two projects both deviate from and follow the Dubai model? To what extent can we say that Cairo is undergoing "Dubaization?"

In 1999 Sheikh Muhammad bin Rashid announced the creation of an IT center called Dubai Internet City (DIC). One year later, with landscaping and high-rises as its finishing touches, the project was complete, and it has become an unqualified success. Occupied by big names in the IT industry, it has made Dubai the IT hub of the region. Comprised of a series of office buildings overlooking an artificial lake and lush gardens, the city is located adjacent to Sheikh Zayed Road. One is led through a gate designed to reflect a traditional wind tower, on to a series of screens that contain a set of "Islamic" motifs, and then to a sequence of glass buildings such as one may find in any high-tech park in Malaysia or Silicon Valley. Although entry is free to anyone (provided they have a car), a protective fence surrounds the project. Located nearby is Media City, a project similar to Internet City, although the occupants here are from the media industry. This "city" is also comprised of office blocks within an artificial landscape. It houses studios and newsrooms and has become a regional center for media companies such as Reuters, CNN, MBC, and others. The anonymity of the office blocks in both of these "cities," which are distinguished only by the logos of their respective inhabitants, highlights the fact that they operate primarily on a global level, in some way disconnected from the surrounding reality.

The Smart Village Project in Cairo is Egypt's attempt to claim the mantle of the region's IT hub. Officials say that it is modeled on similar projects in Ireland and India—countries that have successfully integrated into the global IT service sector. Located along the Cairo-Alexandria desert highway, the 300-acre park will eventually house more than fifty office buildings accommodating 20,000–30,000 employees. Plots of land are offered to potential resident companies, which can then build their own office spaces.[20]

Although Egyptian officials highlight the similarities to the IT and media enclaves in Dubai, the differences between these two ventures are striking. Dubai Internet City is outside of the traditional city on a highway leading to Abu Dhabi. Nevertheless, it is located on a growth corridor and will eventually become a center of the new Dubai, currently under construction. Nearby projects include luxury resorts, the ruler's palace, various gated communities, and the Palm Jumeirah. Driving to DIC, one does not have the feeling of "leaving" Dubai, whereas with Cairo's Smart Village, the sense of leaving Cairo and embarking on a long journey is strong.

An architectural comparison is also insightful. In Dubai, the office blocks are generic buildings that can be found anywhere in the world. In Cairo, an attempt was made to propose buildings with a strong symbolic content, such as a pyramid-shaped café suspended in the middle of a lake or a building whose serially curved shape is suggestive of communication satellites. While Dubai Internet City has added a few vernacular elements (e.g., wind towers and ornaments), the Cairo village main mosque is for some reason constructed using Pharaonic imagery.

Another difference relates to accessibility. In Dubai anyone with a car can enter and walk within the project without interference. The food court is a common meeting place containing a variety of shops and restaurants. It thus integrates quite well, relative to the Cairo project, with the city. In Cairo, entry is through a guarded gate, and subsequent movement within the grounds is closely observed. In both the Dubai and Cairo projects, photography is allowed only after securing permission from authorities, but the DIC has a more flexible attitude. Numbers also show the striking difference between these two centers. While DIC started with more than 200 multinational companies, Smart Village in Cairo has about 58 companies, most of them locally based.[21]

THE CITY CENTER IDEA

The retail sector is one segment where the "Dubai idea" is directly transplanted into an Egyptian context, as evidenced in the Maadi City Center. The Majid Al Futtaim Group of Companies (MAF Group) of Dubai broke ground in mid-November 2001 in the desert outside Cairo for a 22,500-square-meter shopping mall to be anchored by the French food retailer Carrefour. The project, Egypt's first hypermarket, is one of a series of developments by the MAF Group and Carrefour. The partners started the concept in Dubai in 1995 with the Deira City Center, which now receives 50,000 visitors per day and includes such retailers as U.S. department store chain JC Penney and British chains Woolworth's and Marks & Spencer.[22] In addition to the French hypermarket, Cairo's mall includes more than forty shops, several restaurants, and a family entertainment center.

Official accounts suggest the positive impact on Egypt by pointing out that the market will "feature a large range of top quality Egyptian products and international brands targeted to meet the increasing demands of Egyptian consumers."[23] Officials

Entrance to Cairo's Smart Village

Entrance to Cairo's Smart Village

view such a development as a way to modernize Egyptian shopping behavior; the Egyptian Minister of Internal Trade, for example, states:

> A new and civilized marketing approach ... will be introduced to peripheral areas outside of the capital, supplying commodities to small traders seven days a week, 365 days a year. It will supplant the traditional weekly suq (market) held in villages throughout the countryside.[24]

Such efforts are, however, greeted with skepticism in the local media, particularly in light of the failure of a similar venture by the British conglomerate Sainsbury. This case prompted many to call for a radical reorganization of the Egyptian retail sector, described by Sainsbury's chairman as "hostile."[25] Some suggest the possibility of a negative impact on Cairo's small grocery stores: "They've been the staple and the backbone of society for so long they'll never totally disappear, but I think you'll see a lot of them downsizing ... if you can downsize from 75 square meters."[26]

Aside from these economic arguments, one particular area of concern was the cultural acceptance of such a project within an Egyptian context. Although hypermarkets have been socially accepted outside of Egypt, the Egyptian culture may take its time in following the trend.[27] Egyptians will have to choose to spend their free time shopping at Carrefour rather than at smaller, perhaps more conveniently located neighborhood supermarkets. In a culture that highly values a family-oriented and neighborhood-friendly environment, there was skepticism as to whether Egypt would be conducive to hypermarket success. Although the market caters to the nearby upper-middle-class suburb of Maadi, it is aimed at greater Cairo as well. Yet perhaps unbeknown to the project's patrons, long distances and traffic jams may become an insurmountable obstacle. The center's management, however, argues that the mall targets a select clientele: "people coming to us must have a car, so we only cater to a very small percentage of the population. We are here to complement, not compete."[28]

The center is located in an area of Cairo known as Qattamiy'ya at the foot of the Moqatam mountain, near the suburb of Maadi along a highway leading to a recent development named New Cairo. The site is surrounded by empty tracts of land and a large public housing project. The location was chosen specifically to "develop new residential zones," according to the developer. An "example of the type of undeveloped area targeted by the group's development scheme," it thus ties in with what is termed "Carrefour's vision" for Egypt.[29] This vision entails a provision of enough land to accommodate such a complex and extensive areas for parking. Thus the Maadi City Center stands on a 69,000-square-meter parcel, of which 3,500 square meters is Carrefour.[30]

The Egyptian local press largely downplays the Dubai connection and the fact that the center is based on a Dubai model. More emphasis is placed on the French connection, suggesting that Egypt will become Western by constructing centers such as these. According to some observers, "From a shopper's point of view, the shopping center in Qattamiy'ya is perfect. Once you walk inside, you could be anywhere in the world."[31] Accounts in the local Gulf press meanwhile observe that Dubai-based businesses are making inroads into Cairo and other cities as well.

As in Dubai, the center has high design and construction standards and a level of cleanliness not found in other Egyptian malls. The Dubai connection becomes even more apparent given the presence of a UAE-based bank branch. Yet there are also differ-

Entrance to the City Center Mall in Cairo

ences. The most obvious is size. Deira City Center is a large center comprised of multiple levels and several buildings. It occupies the equivalent of several city blocks. In Cairo, the City Center is spread out on one level and is dominated by Carrefour. Another difference pertains to location. In Cairo the Maadi City Center is located at the edge of the city, making it difficult to reach, unlike in Dubai, where Deira City Center is located in the heart of Deira, a commercial and business hub. Deira City Center is, moreover, a major meeting place for city residents; it is also known for always being crowded and catering to a cash-rich, multinational clientele, in addition to locals from Dubai and other emirates.

CONCLUSION

> The flight from Cairo or Beirut to the Gulf states takes only a couple of hours, and in that time the traveler is transported to what might as well be a different planet. He leaves behind a world of decay and dulled tones and steps into one of glitter and dazzle.
> —David Lamb[32]

The above is reflective of a popular viewpoint propagated by journalists and casual observers. Thomas Friedman, for example, maintains that "Dubai is precisely the sort of decent, modernizing model we should be trying to nurture in the Arab-Muslim world."[33] Lee Smith compares Dubai to Baghdad during its Abbasid heyday, because he thinks that the city has reincarnated the ideals of this ancient capital: openness, tolerance, and curiosity. Furthermore, he says that the "Dubai model suggests how the Arab world might revive its historical role as a trade and communications center." In this way, "the Arab world itself becomes a free zone, embracing not only liberal economic policies and new media technologies but eventually political and social reforms." Finally, "what's good for Dubai may in turn be good for the Arab world."[34] The city, according to these viewpoints, should be groomed to become the center for a new Middle East, molded to suit a neoliberal agenda.

Dubai is seemingly becoming a model for urbanism in the Arab world and the center of a "new" Middle East. The relocation of businesses from Cairo to Dubai, visits by Egyptian delegations to learn from Dubai, and laudatory articles in international business publications support this viewpoint. Other cities are influenced as well. Some observers have noted that Beirut has been overshadowed by Dubai, which has assumed the Lebanese capital's mantle as a "gateway to the East." Thus "the legend of the Lebanese gateway to the Middle East, if it were ever based on anything solid, has now attained the status of myth. Economically, at least, the gateway is lying in ruins."[35] The wars in Lebanon, particularly the Israeli offensive of 2006, strengthened Dubai's position. The influence is not, however, restricted to traditional Middle Eastern centers, but extends to Gulf cities as well. Qatar is constructing an island named "the Pearl," modelled on the Palm Islands in Dubai. Similar developments are occurring in Kuwait (City of Silk) and Oman (The Blue City).

Top: Area surrounding the City Center Mall
Bottom: The Sabkha bus stop in Dubai

Although the juxtaposition of slums with luxury developments is not yet as characteristic of Dubai as it is of Amman and, especially, of Cairo, megaprojects and enclaves of the "new Dubai"-type are inherently rife with sociopolitical issues.

In Cairo in 2005, a terrorist alert was issued, based on a specific threat to the Maadi City Center. A security checkpoint was set up at the mall's entrance, and all entering cars were subjected to a search involving bomb-sniffing dogs and guards inspecting cars with mirrors. This continued for many months. Later that year, suicide bombers caused mass havoc in upscale Jordanian hotels. This has led to an ambivalent reaction:

> Those in upscale neighborhoods like Abdoun, for example, have waved flags and festooned their cars with pro-Jordanian banners, while residents of more depressed neighborhoods, like the Palestinian refugee camp at al-Wahdat, have joked that there is finally some benefit to being poor: The attacks occurred in hotels they could never afford to set foot in.[36]

In contrast to Debord's argument about passivity, these events may indicate the emergence of resistance. Resistance, however, is not necessarily violent or confrontational. It can occur, for example, by announcing one's ethnicity through the display of religious symbols, such as the placing of lights in balconies to celebrate the Diwali festival; through the presence of printed street flyers, geared toward compatriots; through the playing of culturally specific sports such as cricket in parking lots; or through the writing of grafitti.

One may argue that Dubai is a model for the Arab world not through its megaprojects but because it accommodates multiple nationalities, which may contribute to its unique response to globalizing conditions. This can be found in the city's forgotten urban public spaces, which I have also termed "transient sites." The discourse on Dubai typically ignores these spaces by focusing instead on the megaprojects.

Such an approach would respond to a shift in global city research, with the emphasis moving toward appreciating uniqueness and differences rather than similarities among cities.[37] This might be termed "globalization from below," but whatever one calls it, it would proceed with a sensitivity to the intimate and dynamic connections between global processes and local lives. It is here that we can learn valuable lessons by looking at Dubai.[38]

Notes

1   Jean Baudrillard, *Simulacra and Simulation* (Ann Arbor: University of Michigan Press, 1995), p. 11.

2   Reuters report, "In Algiers, Traders Do Business the Dubai Way," *Gulf News,* February 14, 2006, p. 41.

3   Guy Debord, *The Society of the Spectacle* (New York: Zone Books, 1995), p. 23. Originally published in 1967 in French.

4   S. Rose, "Sand and Freedom," *The Guardian,* November 28, 2005. *http://arts.guardian.co.uk/features/ story/0,11710,1652149,00.html.* Accessed May 8, 2006.

5   Mike Davis, "Sinister Paradise: Does the Road to the Future End at Dubai?" *Mother Jones,* July 2005, http:// www.motherjones.com/ commentary/columns/2005/07/sinister_paradise. html. Accessed July 11, 2006. This article has since the time of this writing developed into a longer article, "Fear and Money in Dubai," *New Left Review* 41 (Sept., Oct. 2006), pp. 47–68; as well as into a chapter of the book *Evil Paradises: Dreamworlds of Neoliberalism,* Mike Davis and Daniel Bertrand Monk, eds. (New York: New Press, 2007). See also David Harvey, *Spaces of Global Capitalism: Towards a Theory of Uneven Geographical Development* (London: Verso, 2006), p. 13.

6   These statements are from the project's website: http://www.madinatjumeirah.com. Accessed Sept. 2, 2006.

7   Lee Smith, "The Road to Tech Mecca," *Wired* 12, no. 7 (July 2004), http://www.wired.com/wired/ archive/12.07/dubai.html. Accessed Sept. 6, 2006. The scale of Wafi center is insignificant next to the projects planned in the mega-development of Dubailand. Here the pharaonic imagery is taken to fascinating extremes.

8   Since the chapter was written in 2006 much has changed. The tower's name was changed to Burj Khalifa upon its opening in 2010; moreover its height reached 828m. For more information related to recent developments in Dubai, see Y. Eisheshtawny, *Dubai: Behind the Urban Spectacle* (London: Routledge, 2010); also Y. Eisheshtawny, "Little Space/Big Space: Everyday Urbanism in Dubai," *Brown Journal of World Affairs* 17:1.

9   http://www.burjdubai.com. Accessed Sept. 6, 2006.

10   Khaled, a former municipality employee; personal communication, 2004.

11   "Dubai in America: Fake Parks," *The Economist,* July 2006, p. 44.

12   Guy Debord, *Comments on the Society of the Spectacle* (London: Verso, 1998), p. 10.

13   Ibid., p. 50.

14   From the article "The Fast Eat the Slow," *New York Times,* February 2, 2001. http://www.udel.edu/commu-nication/COMM418/begleite/globalagenda/readings/ NYTFriedman020201.html

15   "The Rise of Dubai," *The Economist,* May 27, 2004.

16   A. Lopez-Claros, "The Arab World Competitiveness Report—World Economic Forum" (Hampshire: Palgrave Macmillan, 2005).

17   For a more detailed discussion of the term "Dubaization," see Y. Elsheshtawy, "Reversing Influences: The Dubaization of Cairo," paper presented at UIA ISTANBUL XXII World Congress of Architecture—Cities: Grand Bazaar of Architectures, July 3–7, 2005.

18   "The Rise and Rise of EMAAR Properties," *Arabian Business,* July 23–29, 2006, pp. 34–39.

19   To fully understand the extent of this, see the following newspaper accounts published in 2006 alone: S. Rahman, "EMAAR's Global Operations to Take Lead Role: International Commitments Top $35b," *Gulf News,* March 31, 2006, p. 25; S. Rahman, "EMAAR Signs Three Deals Worth $5.4b in Morocco: Company to Open Country Headquarters in Marakkech," *Gulf News,* March 30, 2006, p. 41; S. Rahman, "Dubai Firms Announce $19b Morocco Projects: Dubai Holding Will Invest $12b and EMAAR $6.9b," *Gulf News,* March 30, 2006, p. 44; S. Husain, "Dubai Project Stimulates Djibouti Economic Growth: Partnership with the Emirate Brings More Investors," *Gulf News,* April 1, 2006, p. 35; S. Husain, "Out of Dubai and Into Africa: Nakheel's Luxury Hotel in Djibouti Set to Welcome First Guests this November," *Gulf News,* April 2, 2006, p. 36.

20   This argument is developed in more detail in Y. Elsheshtawy, "From Dubai to Cairo: Competing Global Cities, Models, and Shifting Centers of Influence?" In *Cairo Cosmopolitan: Politics, Culture, and Space in the New Middle East,* P. Amar and D. Singerman, eds. (Cairo: American University in Cairo Press, 2006), pp. 235–250.

21   http://www.smart-villages.com/default. asp?action=article&ID=27. Accessed Sept. 6, 2006.

22   Information supplied by the centers' websites. Dubai Internet City: http://www.dubaiinternetcity.com/ partner_directory/. Smart Village: http://www.smart-vil-lages.com/default.asp?action=article&ID=31. Accessed Sept. 1, 2006.

23   S. Postlewaite, "FDI Still Apparent: Gulf Investors Stay Despite Capital Flight," *Business Monthly Online,* November, 2001.

24   N.A., "Majid Al-Futaim Starts Egypt Project,"*Gulf News Online Edition,* November 30, 2001. http://www.gulf-news.com/Articles/news.asp?ArticleID=34053. Accessed 21/9/05.

25   A. Sami, "Supermarketing Hysterics," *Al-Ahram Weekly Online,* April 19–25, 2001. http://weekly.ahram.org. eg/2001/530/ec1.htm. Accessed 23/9/05

26   Ibid.

27   T. Hinde, "Interview" *Business Today Online,* February, 2003. http://www.businesstodayegypt.com/default. aspx?IssueID=116. Accessed July 2003.

28   H. Rashdan, "Egypt Gets Hyper," *Al-Ahram Weekly Online,* January 30–February 5, 2003. http://weekly. ahram.org.eg/2003/623/li1.htm, Accessed Sept. 23, 2005.

29   Ibid., and Hinde, "Interview."

30   Ibid., and Rashdan, "Egypt Gets Hyper."

31   Hinde, "Interview."

32   Ibid.

33   David Lamb, *The Arabs: Journeys Beyond the Mirage* (New York: Vintage, 2002), p. 34.

34   T. Friedman, "Dubai and Dunces," *New York Times,* March 15, 2006. http://select.nytimes.com/2006/03/15/ opinion/15friedman.html. Accessed, Sept. 7, 2006.

35   Smith, "The Road to Tech Mecca."

36   D. Champion, "Does the Gateway to the Middle East Lie in Ruins? Golden Days Seem Far Away," *The Daily Star Online,* Feb. 10, 2004. http://www.dailystar.com.lb. Accessed Sep. 21, 2005

37   M. Slackman and M. el-Naggar, "A Saddened, But Ambivalent, Jordan Muses on Bombings' Aftermath," *International Herald Tribune,* Nov. 18, 2005, p. 5.

38   Elsheshtawy, "From Dubai to Cairo."

AHMED KANNA

9

DUBAI, IN PARTICULAR: ANOMALOUS SPACES AND IGNORED HISTORIES IN THE "SUPERLATIVE CITY"

Dubai has seized the imagination of the wider world. While certainly photogenic, this hypermodern city of shopping malls and resort enclaves may in fact tell us more about what urban scholars like Anne-Marie Broudehoux have called "urban entrepreneurialism" than it does about the city as a more complex phenomenon and its other, less visible, lived realities.[1] Urban entrepreneurialism, also known as "place wars," is characterized by rise of spectacle and competition for superlative distinction among cities at the start of the twenty-first century. Emerging or "wannabe" global cities are especially fixated on the spectacular:

"Old Dubai." Dubai Museum seen from the fifth floor of the Arabian Courtyard hotel

> Wannabe cities are ... cities of intense urban redevelopment, and cities with pow-
> erful growth rhetoric. They also have an edgy insecurity about their roles and
> position in the world that gives tremendous urgency to their cultural boosterism.
> The desperate scramble for big name architects, art galleries and cultural events
> is a fascinating part of the 'place wars' amongst cities aiming for the top of the
> urban hierarchy.[2]

In the case of cities such as Beijing and Dubai, this boosterism has been wildly successful. Not that long ago, many people would have struggled to locate Dubai on a
map. Dubai's increased profile owes not a little to the reception and dissemination of
the city's image in the Western press, which tends, politically and economically, to see
the world in a neoliberal sort of way. Almost none of the Western mass media seem to
be aware, for example, of Dubai's approximately century-old transnational identity as
a hub between Africa, the Middle East, and South Asia. These media equate "transna-
tionalism" with neoliberal globalization and they judge Dubai accordingly. Thus Dubai
becomes the exceptional Arab city, the city where Arabs show that they are capable
of moving beyond "antiquated" ideas such as nationalism and socialism, a forward-
looking place that is "about nurturing Arab dignity through success not suicide."[3]
This narrative tempts us to dissolve Dubai's concrete reality, as the anthropologist
Marshall Sahlins might say, in the acid bath of teleology, that of capitalism as a mono-
lithic phenomenon progressively encompassing or occupying the whole of the world,
regardless of the agency, resistances, or appropriations of local peoples deploying
localized structures of meaning.

In this chapter, I focus on Dubai's particularity, not as an argument that we should
extract the city from global contexts of capitalism or great power politics, but as a corrective to top-down, reductive analyses that select out only the data that confirm their
globalizing assumptions. This chapter is a kind of superficial tour of some of the Dubai
spaces that are located more specifically in memories and urbanities preceding—in
the temporal, not the evolutionary sense—the images of today's advertising campaigns and journalistic coverage.[4] These memories and urbanities help give modernity
its specific shape in Dubai.

By contrasting, in the following observations, the Dubai state's (especially the
ruler, Muhammad bin Rashid's) almost classical modernist space to the discursive
and practical spaces of everyday Dubayyans, I am drawing on a distinction made by
Henri Lefebvre. In works such as *The Urban Revolution* and *The Production of Space*,
Lefebvre contrasts the reductive, abstract spatial logic of states and other institutions
of power with the more diverse lived spaces of everyday people. The former, what
Lefebvre calls "abstract space," seeks to dominate space and populations, seeing the
world as a target for instrumental ordering and calculability. The latter, what he calls
"differential space," escapes from this administrative will and resides in the fragmentary diversity of everyday life.[5] For Lefebvre, differential space can be a literal space
or something more figurative: a performance, a reworking of centralizing, official
discourses, or a repressed memory of space or a spatial relation. As Theodor Adorno—

with whose work Lefebvre's insights into modern space strongly resonate—may have put it: differential space cannot be reduced to the logic and conceptual apparatus of administration.

This chapter is therefore a survey of some differential spaces of Dubai—spaces, whether literal or figurative, that cannot be reduced to the administrative, instrumental logic of neoliberal reasoning. I first analyze what I think of as one of the representative spaces of power in Dubai, the abstract, arguably modernist space of Sheikh Muhammad's Nakheel project, the Palm Jebel Ali. I then look at how local discourses, history, and practices differentially relate to and trouble the modernist assumptions applied from the outside or top-down by elites. Although the focus here is on what might be termed the ignored or anomalous spaces of Dubai, this is not to take Dubai out of a global reality of capitalism and empire. Local urban process emerges within a field already delimited by historical forces that advance neoliberal politics, urbanity, consumption, and sociality, yet is not reducible to these forces.[6]

HIGH MODERNISM REDUX?

Architectural criticism of Dubai is a good example of the analytical selectivity and neoliberal bias of Western representations of the city. These discussions often ignore or minimize the fact that Dubai is an absolutist monarchy, opting instead for a technocratic and depoliticized presentation of architectural form. By taking at face value the spectacular aspects of the city, this tendency risks ignoring the deeply political nature of practices of spatial abstraction and aesthetic excess in Dubai architecture. Although Dubai architects do have room to negotiate the form of urban projects, ultimately they have to realize the ruler's or the landlord's desired image. In Dubai, architectural projects tend to be both immense and sculptural. A good example is the Palm Jebel Ali. On the surface, this seems to be classic postmodern resort enclave, and indeed, elements of this style and urban approach are evident. It is more revealing, however, to point out the similarities to modernist space, especially as this pertains to state domination.

For example, the project is literally an expression of the sovereignty of the absolute monarch, Muhammad bin Rashid. A land barrier surrounding the peninsular form of the project will be built up from reclaimed land in the shape of the Arabic script of one of the ruler's poems:

Take wisdom from the wise
It takes a man of vision to write on water
Not everyone who rides a horse is a jockey
Great men rise to greater challenges

This project is so enormous that a person on the ground cannot get a sense of it; it can only be fully comprehended from an airplane. The size of the project, and the fact that the ruler views it as a means to literally inscribe his authority onto the space of the city, suggests a monumental, propagandistic intent. In this sense, the Sheikh is not unlike the baroque princes described by Lewis Mumford, who saw themselves as genius-planners and artists of the city.[7] The Palm Jebel Ali, moreover, is a typical if extreme version of Dubai's monumentalism. Like modernist urban design with its sculptural solids in vast, empty spaces, this monumentalism exhibits an almost purely aesthetic approach.[8] As James Scott has pointed out, this approach has its roots in the early modern era of Europe: "the baroque redesigning of medieval cities, with its grand edifices, vistas, squares, and attention to uniformity, proportion, and perspective, was intended to reflect the grandeur and awesome power of the prince."[9]

Two other aspects of the Palm Jebel Ali are also standard features of modernism: the project's scale and its obsession with order. The "geometric order" that high modernism imposes on the landscape, says Scott, "is most evident, not at street level, but rather from above and from outside." It is, "in short, a God's-eye view, or the view of an absolute ruler."[10] Second, although superficially a mixed-use development, the Palm Jebel Ali envisions something like the "death of the street." In a confluence of modernism and new urbanism, notions such as strolling and a diverse, active street life are planned out of the Palm Jebel Ali and the other enclaves that now dominate the city's urban scape. In its size, its subordination of the average person on the street, and its functional segregation, the Palm Jebel Ali is more Radiant City than Disneyworld. Yet rather than signaling Dubai's total absorption into this kind of modernity, this aesthetic vision encounters in the lived reality of the city's inhabitants many points of slippage where modernist abstraction, whether spatial (as in the case of the Palm Jebel Ali, etc.) or conceptual (as in that of the aforementioned neoliberals), is either interrupted or negotiated by local discourses or appropriations.

SPECTERS

About 60 kilometers along the Gulf coast northeast of Dubai is the emirate of Ras al-Khayma, in which stand the ruins of a substantial old town center. At 2–3 square kilometers, it is surprisingly large and resembles what the old town center of Dubai looked like until about fifteen years ago. Coral and mud walls have crumbled and stand in piles within the courtyards or in the narrow alleys that run between the houses.

Embellishments such as arched niches and engravings on overhangs attest to a lost urban grandeur, giving clues to the historical situation of villages such as Ras al-Khayma and Dubai as ports that sustained a trading elite connected to other ports on the littoral of the Persian Gulf and Indian Ocean. Ironically, Dubai's rise was made possible when the British, in the early nineteenth century, levelled Ras al-Khayma because they viewed it as a base for pirates. The British went on to support and secure Dubai as an alternative power base in the lower Gulf. One wonders how much of Ras al-Khayma's current dilapidation was a result of the British deciding that the town was a "capital of piracy." In Dubai's old center, the Bastakiyya, an Iranian merchant elite had established a community in the early part of the twentieth century. "We traded, we bought and sold, and we were happy," I am told by an elderly man who remembers the days before *al-madina al-mu'awlama* (the global city).

Top: Exterior wall of courtyard house in Ras
al-Khayma, United Arab Emirates
Middle: Courtyard of the former house of a
wealthy merchant family, Ras al-Khayma
Bottom: Wooden door, Ras al-Khayma, with the
inscription "1376" (AH), or 1956 CE

In the courtyard of a large, finely embellished house in Ras al-Khayma, one now finds rubble, as if the place has been bombed. This lost urban form is grist for the mill both of folk narratives recounting recent UAE history and for the various emirates' emerging heritage revival projects. Semi-official and official Imarati Arabic-language newspapers, for example, commonly feature philosophical essays or poems eulogizing the times gone by. The following example is typical:

> It is indubitable that the beautiful, simple life that is lived in quiet, cleanliness, and vitality, and which has inexorably receded from our modern lives, characterized the old town with its cooperative, harmonious society, just as it characterized the cooperative, harmonious countryside (al-rif al-muta'awin wa-l-mutakafil).[11]

During my research, most Imaratis to whom I spoke reflected in similar ways about the times that have passed and Dubai's transformation from a "village" (qarya), where life was hard but everyone supposedly knew and helped everyone else, to a "cosmopolitan city" (madina 'alamiyya) or "global city" (madina mu'awlama), rich in both creature comforts and dangers. An Imarati architect reflected upon a suburb of Dubai:

> There is an interesting area called Mishrif. It's all Bedouins (i.e., ethnically Arab Imarati nationals).[12] Actually, everyday, there is a women's majlis (formal reception), for the whole area. All the women will come. . . they really know each other, this wife knows the other wife and knows her daughters and they see each other. But now [in most parts of Dubai], you don't have that, because I'm living next to somebody I don't know, and he's living next to a guy he doesn't know.[13]

Suffering and melancholy are frequently expressed in discourses of cultural alienation or Kafkaesque bureaucratization. Sections of Arabic newspapers contain not only philosophical reflections on the qarya, but fictional tales allegorizing a present in which one feels stranded (as historian Peter Fritzsche might put it).[14] "This story recurs every six months," begins a typical one. An elderly woman carries a pile of paperwork to a government office, where she is to apply for the state welfare program for widows. "Where is Khalid, the young man who usually sits here?" she asks. "Khalid has gone on annual holiday," a disembodied voice tells her. The widow asks the speaker if he can help her. "I can't do anything until you show me court papers proving that you are a widow ... and papers proving the passing of the deceased ... and witnesses' proof of this ... and the names of the neighbors that visit you ... and your sons' papers ... and those of their wives ... and ... and ... and ..." She has filled all the correct papers, "but because of the absence of one bureaucrat she was required to submit to a new process for everything (ihsa'iyya jadida likulli-shay')."[15]

The Dubai municipality decided in 1996 to renovate the Bastakiyya, under the banner of "heritage preservation" of the "cultural identity" of the city.[16] The municipality began a survey of the district and its approximately fifty wind-tower houses. The survey's analysis of the population noted that the Bastakiyya had once been inhabited by wealthy families who had the means to maintain the old buildings. Unfortunately, these families had moved to new districts during the oil period (*al-hiqba al-naftiyya*) of the 1970s.[17] Thus the district was left for "classes of limited income," who also happened to be foreigners. Accompanying this observation, written up in a summary of the survey called "a historical fragment of the Bastakiyya" published by the Dubai municipality, is a photo of the façade of an abandoned courtyard house, in front of which stands an Asian man. The caption reads: "Expatriate Asian workers living in one of the buildings. Note the presence of changes attendant to their settling in the building, for example, the air conditioners and electrical light units." The report adds: "Naturally, [these foreign workers] are not conscious of the importance of the architectural heritage that surrounds them and they do not have the means to care for it."[18]

The juxtaposition of the specific temporality—the break with the past, society entering a new, uncertain period of social anomie—and of an ethnicized conception of national belonging is not accidental. Historian James Onley, in his study of Gulf Arab national dress, makes the argument that before the oil era, the people of the Gulf saw their identity as multinational and multiethnic, a pluralistic attitude most vividly captured in the local dress of the pre-oil era, an amalgam of African, Arab, Iranian, and Indian elements.[19] Only after the oil boom, when the influx of foreigners began to overwhelm the locals, did local dress, and by extension, according to Onley, local identity, become "Arabized," jettisoning Persian, Indian, and African elements and adopting an overwhelmingly Arabian (specifically, a Najdi) character.

It is at this point that the past becomes "the Past," unreachably remote from the present, separated from the contemporary situation by a break. The local terms for this past is often *ayyam al-ajdad*, "the days of our grandfathers," or *al-ayyam al-sabqa*, simply, "the passed/past days." This was a time when life was supposedly more harmonious, when "our backs were tired but our hearts were at peace," as an elderly Imarati told

Left: Renovated courtyard of the house of wealthy trading family, Bastakiyya, Dubai
Right: Steps leading down into a Bastakiyya courtyard, pre-renovation

me (*fi'l-ayyam al-sabqa, kinna ta'banin bass galbna kan mirtah*). The barrier that emerges between ethnicities and between the past and the present appears at the point at
which the UAE becomes far more intensely integrated into the global economy. These
boundaries are what enable the Imaratis to locate themselves within modernity. The
rebirth of the Bastakiyya, its historical imperfections whitewashed and plastered over,
is a good example of the official absorption of the city's built heritage into the projects
of modern state-building and heritage revival, examples of the state's aforementioned
modernist spatial logic. Like the whitewashing of the Bastakiyya's façades, which erases
the process of the buildings' construction, the contemporary conversion of the old
houses into high-rent retail, hotel, and restaurant spaces erases the memory of the lived
historical reality of the district as residence of the old town's Persian merchant elite.

The "new Dubai" of the shopping malls, palm-shaped resorts, and heritage preservation sites is an urban scape that marginalizes the ambivalences in a story that is only
apparently one of progressive triumph and prosperity. In reality, the story is more complex, lacking any simple or edifying message.

MOBILITY

Neoliberalism idealizes a world of global flows, the supposedly unfettered mobility
of goods and peoples. Dubai appeals to exponents of this theory because it appears
to enable such unmediated movement. In the view of Friedman and other Western
boosters of Dubai, this alleged quality makes the city-state exceptional in the Arab and
Middle Eastern contexts, an enclave in which the free market rules. The city's prosperity, in this view, is proof that the statist and rentier economies of the surrounding Arab
countries have failed. The case of Dubai is seen to confirm the neoliberal maxim that
the state should be kept away from the market as much as possible. Nicholas Kristof,
another booster, critiqued anti-Dubai voices in the United States during the "Dubai
ports scandal" of early 2006 with this revealing comment: "Secretary of State Cordell
Hull used to say that 'when goods do not cross borders, armies do.'"[20] For Kristof, "free
trade" prevents conflict and can (and should) be divorced from political intervention.

These writers assume a neat dividing line between sectors of the economy in
which the state intervenes and others free from state intervention. Liberal economic
theory suggests that the latter is a pure sphere that is (or should be) kept free from
politics; political intervention, it is asserted, is irrational or illegitimate, corrupting the
sanctity of unfettered economic activity. As many anthropologists, including Carolyn
Nordstrom argue, however, it is more productive to think of the economy not as separate from society and politics but as part of a larger sociopolitical and cultural context.
Nordstrom, maintains that we should think in terms of the "total" or "real economy."[21]
Dubai is favorably situated at the center of a region that, since the 1970s, has been
experiencing wars (Lebanon, Iraq, Iran, Afghanistan, Yugoslavia, the USSR), neoliberal
restructuring (the USSR, India, former African clients of the USSR), and attempted (and
sometimes successful) religious insurrections (Iran, Saudi Arabia, Pakistan). The movement of goods and people through Dubai depends both on the political instability

and difficult transitions in the emerging capitalist economies surrounding it, and on the ways in which the city's political class responds to and guides these movements through their borders. For example, almost none of Dubai's most profitable sectors, such as shipping, construction, and *hawala* (non-traceable money transfers), are entirely, if at all, formal. As the case of the construction workers defrauded from promised wages or simply pressed into effective wage slavery attests, profits (to labor agents, labor camp managers, and other profiteers) and savings (to employers) in the labor market are deeply political, based on the connections of those who control capital to the state.[22] Second, Dubai is a polity in which up to 90 percent of the population is foreign: its prosperity, more than that of most other societies, fundamentally depends on the selective, political interventions of the state in movements of people. Visa regulations, tourism policies, corporate laws, and labor control regimes all tend to be relatively laissez-faire with regard to wealthier North American and European expatriates and much more strict and interventionist in relation to poorer South Asian, Middle Eastern, etc., expatriates.

In other respects as well, the real economy of Dubai is one from which political intervention cannot be dissociated, whether the case is smuggling, a main source of income for the pre-oil emirate and an activity in which the rulers colluded, or the redoubtable free-trade zones of contemporary Dubai, enclaves created by the state to permit corporations to operate under exceptional legal frameworks.[23] These mundane facts of the economic life of a transshipment hub are sometimes exoticized, rendered as "smuggling," "organized crime," or "state corruption." But, as Nordstrom puts it:

> Shipping routes are markets, and thus they are matters of opportunity. The number of markets and routes to these marketplaces is not unlimited. Once routes are operating with confidence, all manner of goods can pass along them. A shipping container can "contain" arms, cigarettes, and the latest pirated DVDs, along with a host of other commodities ranging from the seriously illegal to the merely mundane ... such transits work more smoothly than they would if all routes were separate: arms buyers find an easy market for cigarettes, videos, and information technology (or Mach 3 razors, 4 X 4 all-terrain vehicles, or pornography).[24]

So-called smuggling and informal economies, then, should not be abstracted from the total or real economy. Dubai, along with Hong Kong, Singapore, Rotterdam, and a few other hubs, is one of the world's major shipping centers. By 2004, Dubai was the world's tenth largest transshipment hub, handling 6.4 million twenty-foot equivalent units (TEUs, a standard transshipment unit of volume).[25] "More than 90 percent of world trade is conducted by the international shipping industry. Around 50,000 ships registered in 150 countries are manned by more than a million sailors from virtually every country in the world." Moreover, "the most sophisticated ports in the world can inspect a maximum of only 5 percent of the cargo passing through customs."[26]

Thus regional economic and political conditions shape the specific form of the transshipment and re-export economies of Dubai. Specific policies—for example, those pertaining to, say, deregulation in Russia, offshore banking in Saudi Arabia or Iran, or marketization of the state sector in Nigeria—and the local political regime in Dubai are indissociable from the city's economic life. Other political factors are also worth considering. Port cities such as Dubai depend on imperial umbrellas to function as safe havens for fleeing regional and transnational capital. The British ensured the primacy of shipping centers such as Aden and Singapore in their imperial heyday. The transfer from British to American naval command on the Indian Ocean island of Diego Garcia in the 1970s was a change of the guard, but the pattern remained unchanged. Now the Americans provide the military umbrella that ensures "free trade" in the region. In 2005, outside of Iraq, there were approximately 36,660 American troops in the Gulf, 25,250 of which were in Kuwait, with Bahrain, Qatar, and the UAE accounting for most of the remainder.[27] While millions of average Iraqis were killed or displaced by the American occupation, the wealthier among them simply transferred operations to places like Amman and Dubai. Meanwhile, consumer goods regularly arrived in Iraqi markets, almost always informally, by way of Dubai.[28]

Dubai's shoehorning into prevailing, Western notions of globalization is most limiting, however, when we attempt to understand the city's Indian Ocean context, a story of other globalizations both conceptually and spatially distant from neoliberal understandings of transnational interconnection.[29] It is not uncommon for Imaratis of earlier generations, who would be in their sixties or older today, to switch effort-lessly between Arabic, Persian, Swahili, and Urdu or Hindi. For many of these people, life before the economic boom of the 1970s was regulated by the seasons and the seas. Every December, they took a hiatus from fishing and sailed the rim of the Indian Ocean, stopping off in places like Aden, Mombasa, Zanzibar, Basra, and Bombay, and picking up a variety of goods, idioms, and food customs, and perhaps marrying local women as well. The southwest monsoon carried them back in April, and Dubai's market would suddenly be transformed into an emporium where the goods mapped the convolutions of *Pax Britannica*: coffee from Yemen, rice from Burma, barley and dates from Iran and Iraq, and spices, metals, and timber from India.[30] Political instabilities in larger sur-rounding states were beneficial to these small port towns, which supplied neighboring countries with the goods made unavailable by border closings or expulsions of trad-ers. Even conflicts seemingly remote from this corner of Southern Arabia caused local reverberations. In the late 1940s, for example, as the frontiers between Pakistan and India closed, Dubai sailor merchants brought Pakistani goods to Dubai and resold them to India, and vice versa.[31]

Along with being an entrepot, Dubai was until the middle of the twentieth century a tiny and remote locale in the hinterland of the Raj, integrated into and suppressed by the British Empire via treaties securing access to India. Therefore, uniquely for a town within the conventional boundaries of the Arab world, Dubai's identity was strongly Perso-South Asian and African. The UAE (what were known as the Trucial States under the British) were among the small handful of Arab territories that the British ruled from Calcutta, not from Cairo.

A standard source on the early twentieth-century Gulf thus tells us that around 1915 there were 250 Persian houses to the 440 Arab houses in the town.[32] Along with the Persians and Arabs, about 5 percent of the town's population of 10,000 in 1915 were African and South Asian: Sudanese, Baluchis, Hindus, and Khojas (Muslims from the Bombay area).

James Onley summarizes the connection between mobility and cultural identity in the pre-oil, pre-neoliberalizing Gulf:

> Many Gulf Arab men had Persian, Indian, or African wives, and their children spoke Farsi, Urdu, Baluchi, Hindi or Swahili, along with Arabic. Many went to study in India. The Gulf Arabs ate lamb and fish with Indian curried rice. In all these aspects and many more besides, the ports and the peoples of Eastern Arabia belonged more to the Indian Ocean than to the Arab world.[33]

In this context, memorial discourses about the vanished village can be seen as mnemonics for a place and time not antecedent to the current period of globalization but which presented an alternative, now officially forgotten cosmopolitanism and transnationality.[34]

URBANITY

Do Dubai's forgotten histories manifest themselves in areas outside of discourse? Although numerous parts of the city have yet to be subjected entirely to the simplifications and legibility of the neoliberal-sheikhly state, the area where such spaces are most densely concentrated are around the Creek, and neighborhoods such as Satwa, Karama, Nasser Square, and Khalid ibn-al-Walid Street (also known as "Bank Street"); and old markets and shopping thoroughfares such as the gold suq, the Deira fish and vegetable market, and al-Dhiyafa Street.[35] In these neighborhoods the city does not exhibit the God's-eye scaling or the functional segregation of the ideal modern Euro-American city and its "new Dubai" avatar. On the contrary, the symbolic, the mercantile, and the public are complexly intertwined.

This Dubai is best accessed on foot, not by car. Beginning at the great symbolic center of the area, the Al Maktum mosque, one notices immediately that Islam and Hinduism, the Arab world and the Indian Ocean, are represented here. A cosmopolitanism is referenced that has its symbolic center not only in Mecca or Cairo but also in Bombay and Cochin and, indeed, in Dubai itself, a world where religions, mono- and polytheistic, intermingle in ways that would strike a Cairene or a Levantine (to say nothing of a Westerner) as radically different from the norm. Tucked just next to the mosque is the Hindu Temple of Dubai, which locals and expatriates both sometimes (incorrectly) point out as the Arab world's only such temple. The temple anchors a shaded court ringed by small shops, kiosks, and cafés. Snaking behind mosque and temple is a system of narrow alleys and nooks that form something of a focal point of urban Indian culture in Dubai.

Left: Square near the Al Maktoum mosque and Dubai's Hindu Temple
Right: Alley near the Al Maktoum mosque

Street signage here also tells the story of regionally specific, transnational cultural mixing. Arabic, English, and Hindi script appear on signs. Posters advertise Hindu religious ceremonies and varied social services. After lunchtime, when the grocery and textile shops on the Temple Square shut down, men nap on benches. Nearby, on a street with high-rises all around, it is common to see workers from Pakistan or Afghanistan, wearing *qamizshirwals*, sitting on a pull-carts or benches, playing cards. The street remains alive.

Across the Creek, in the area of the gold suq, one can find a similar intermingling of the symbolic, the mercantile, and the informal, such as tiny mosques (*masajid*) tucked into the crevices of the complex network of shops and cafés. People may be just as likely use the space of the masjid for a nap as they would for prayer. Such mixed behavioral geographies can be seen everywhere, where narrow, socially rich spaces that are convoluted and illegible in the eyes of the neoliberal state accommodate activities that are not "designed" into these spaces, as when a soccer game or a cricket match breaks out in the interstitial areas of Satwa or Jumeirah. Such spaces may be "illegible" and "complex" from the perspective of the state or of top-down planning, but from the perspective of their inhabitants, they make sense and are quite legible.

The cultural mixing presented in these spaces is another example of Dubai's situation at the crossroads of Iran, South Asia, and the Arab countries, and this is reflected in everyday peoples' experience.[36] For example, an Imarati and an Indian independently told me how both nationalities have long shared South Asian lingua francas and cultural referents. Both remembered going in the 1980s to the only movie theater (they claimed) then in Dubai, which showed Bollywood films. The Imaratis had no problem following the subtitle-free stories, according to my informants. There are other, even more contemporary examples: Indian TV series set in Dubai narrating, and naturalizing, Dubai Indian love triangles and conspicuous consumption; and popular Arabic-

Left: Gold Suq area, Deira
Right: Kids in Satwa

language shows depicting Imarati and Indian protagonists communicating in Hindi. Indians often say that the streets of Dubai, with their embarrassment of riches in Indian restaurants and cafés, Diwali festivals, and tens of thousands of Indian expatriates, are a place where "you really don't feel like you're away from home."

Two final examples will show the ways in which modernization, rather than dominating or homogenizing spaces and attitudes, is inflected by local structures of meaning in contemporary Dubai. Several Imarati woman informants told me that the homogeneity, the surveillance, and in general, the modernity of the shopping mall makes such spaces more inviting than street-facing cafés. Elements such as enclosure and predictability create a space where women do not mind being seen unaccompanied. They see malls as places for everyone, whereas street cafés are too male-dominated and open; one is too visible to the street there, and Imarati women are concerned about maintaining their *sum'a*, or reputation, for not mixing with strange men. In the regulated and surveilled ("climatized," in Baudrillard's words) context of the shopping mall, Imarati women feel less threatened by the potential gaze or physical proximity of men. Far from being an alienating, homogeneously modern space advancing Western cultural imperialism, a common complaint of anti-globalization voices both within the UAE and without, the mall becomes appropriated in specific ways by local people for local agendas.

The hypermarket of Deira City Center shopping mall is the context for such placemaking in the case of an Imarati bureaucrat who guided me through local culture during my research. Although thankful for what he calls his country's *tahaddur* (the "modernization" or "civilization" brought about by oil wealth), he feels that people have lost a sense of solidarity and purpose. Now they mostly go to the malls, hang out at Starbucks, and talk about cars, mobile phones, and "frivolous things." He fears that his children will begin to lose their identity entirely. He attempts to head off this eventuality by taking them to Carrefour, the French hypermarket anchoring the Deira City Center, and giving them a tour of the fish section. He focuses on the local fish, which he teaches his sons to distinguish from non-indigenous varieties while telling them stories about how Imaratis depended on fishing before the *hiqba naftiyya* and the *madina mu'awlama*.

One should not romanticize such examples or mistake them for "creativity" or the resilience of local culture in the face of a dynamic and powerful capitalism. Global capitalism, in its present incarnation as neoliberalim, and local worlds coexist and are in constant dialectical tension. It is not that there are two distinct realities, one capitalist, global, and cosmopolitan, the other local, illegible, and mysterious. As the example of Imarati women at shopping malls and my friend's fish story suggest, Western-style Capitalist modernization provides the spatial and material substrates through which localized desires, ideals, and spatial appropriations become active. These examples, as well as the discourses of memory and the lived spaces of the city mentioned earlier, show that our definition of cities quite literally depends on our perspective. When we look at the world from the perch of a self-styled economic theorist, the world comes to appear populated by data either confirming or deviating from our preconceived notions about urban form and social behavior. When we descend onto the street and engage the ground-level realities, the city begins to slip out from the embrace of our concepts. It is this ground-level, experiential dimension of urban life, with all its reappropriations and negotiations of abstract, quantifying logic, that makes urban life so dynamic and irreducible.

Notes

1   Anne-Marie Broudehoux, "Spectacular Beijing: The Conspicuous Construction of an Olympic Metropolis," *Journal of Urban Affairs,* vol. 29, no. 4 (2007), pp. 383–399.

2   John Rennie Short, *Urban Theory: A Critical Assessment* (New York: Palgrave MacMillan, 2006), p. 115.

3   Thomas Friedman, "Dubai and Dunces" *New York Times*, March 15, 2006; see also *The Economist*, "Beyond Oil," A *Survey of the Gulf*, March 23, 2002, pp. 26–28; Ibrahim al-Malifi, "*Dubai: Iqtisad al-Ma'rifa wa thawrat al-Midia wa'-l-Ma'lumatiyya* (Dubai: The Information Economy and the Media and Communications Revolution), *al-Arabi* 524, July 2002, pp. 100–109; Seth Sherwood, "The Oz of the Middle East," *New York Times*, May 8, 2005, accessed at http://travel2.nytimes.com/2005/05/08/travel/08dubai.html on October 13, 2008.

4   Those interested in more detailed ethnographic or historical accounts of Dubai may consult Neha Vora, *Impossible Citizens: Dubai's Indian Diaspora* (Durham, NC: Duke University Press, 2013); Christopher Davidson, *Dubai: The Vulnerability of Success* (New York: Columbia University Press, 2008), and Ahmed Kanna, *Dubai, The City as Corporation* (Minneapolis: University of Minnesota Press, 2011).

5   See Henri Lefebvre, *The Production of Space*, D. Nicholson-Smith, trans. (Malden, MA: Blackwell, 1991), and *The Urban Revolution*, R. Bononno, trans. (Minneapolis: University of Minnesota Press, 2003).

6   For an elaboration on my analysis of Dubai as a neoliberalizing city, see A. Kanna, "Dubai in a Jagged World," *Middle East Report* 243 (Summer 2007), pp. 22–29, and A. Kanna and A. Keshavarzian, "The UAE's Space Race: Sheikhs and Starchitects Envision the Future," *Middle East Report* 248 (Fall 2008), pp. 34–39. By anomalous, I mean literally "without a name," as the Greek root of the term suggests. From the perspective of what Dipesh Chakrabarty calls the "life process" of capital, spaces, times, and practices that are outside of or do not enable this life process are incapable of being named; they are assumed not to exist. Dipesh Chakrabarty, "Two Histories of Capital," in D. Chakrabarty, *Provincializing Europe: Postcolonial Thought and Historical Difference* (Princeton: Princeton University Press, 2000), pp. 47–71.

7   Lewis Mumford, The City in History: Its Origins, Its Transformations, and Its Prospects (New York: Harcourt, Brace, and World, 1961), pp. 344–374.

8   As James Holston argues, the modernist emphasis on sculptural architecture has had serious

consequences for how people experience buildings and the urban landscape, giving modernist space its monumental, sometimes superhuman proportions. See Holston's *The Modernist City: An Anthropological Critique of Brasilia* (Chicago: University of Chicago Press, 1989), pp. 119–127.

9   James C. Scott, *Seeing Like a State: How Certain Schemes to Improve the Human Condition Have Failed* (New Haven: Yale University Press, 1998), p. 56.

10   Ibid., p. 57.

11   Dr. Mahmud Shahin, *"al-Rif: Milathth al-Ruh al-Ma'zuma waWasadat-al-Ra's al-Mut'aba"* ("The Country: Delight of the Exhausted Spirit and Cushion to the Weary Head"), *al-Bayan*, May 7, 2004. My translation.

12   As opposed to "Persian" Imaratis, descendants of Iranian immigrants who have become naturalized Imaratis. See Kanna, "The State Philosophical," pp. 59–73.

13   Interview with "Yusuf Khalil," a Dubayyan architect, June 2004. Conducted in English. I deal at length and in great detail with these idyllic discourses of the vanished village in my recently published book, *Dubai, The City as Corporation*.

14   Peter Fritzsche, *Stranded in the Present: Modern Time and the Melancholy of History* (Cambridge: Harvard University Press, 2004).

15   Sultan al-Ka'aby, *"Mu'ana 'Ajuz* (The Sufferings of an Old Woman)," *al-Ittihad*, June 19, 2004. My translation. Example taken from Kanna, *"Not Their Fathers' Days,"* p. 135.

16   Aftab Kazmi, "Conservation Plan Proposed for Dubai's Bastakiyya District," *Gulf News*, April 14, 2004.

17   For example, Mishrif, Za'abeel, Jumeirah.

18   *"Nubdha tarikhiyya 'an mantiqat-al-bastakiyya"* ("Historical Fragment on the Bastakiyya District"), n.d., Dubai Municipality. My translation.

19   Oil was discovered at different times in various Gulf countries. In the UAE, oil was first struck in 1958 in Abu Dhabi. Most Gulf countries became dramatically wealthier after the OPEC oil embargo of 1973. James Onley, "Gulf Arab Headdress Before Oil: A Study in Cultural Diversity and Hybridity." Panel Paper, Middle East Studies Association Annual Conference, San Francisco, November 2004. See also Fredrick Anscombe, "An Anational Society: Eastern Arabia in the Ottoman Period," in Madawi al-Rasheed, ed., *Transnational Connections and the Arab Gulf* (New York: Routledge, 2005).

20   Nicholas Kristof, "The Arabs Are Coming," *New York Times*, February 26, 2006.

21   Carolyn Nordstrom, *Global Outlaws: Crime, Money, and Power in the Contemporary World* (Berkeley: University of California Press, 2007).

22   See "Building Towers, Cheating Workers," *Human Rights Watch*, November 2006, vol. 18, no. 8(E).

23   Aihwa Ong has called the latter "graduated sovereignty," a practice in which states selectively apply their domination or control over territories and populations in response to shifting market pressures. Aihwa Ong, "Graduated Sovereignty in Southeast Asia," *Theory, Culture & Society*, vol. 17, no. 4 (2000), pp. 55–75. Reprinted in Ong, *Neoliberalism as Exception* (Durham: Duke University Press, 2007).

24   Nordstrom, *Global Outlaws*, p. 8.

25   Eric Heymann, "Container Shipping," *Deutsche Bank Research*, April 25, 2006, p. 13.

26   Nordstrom, *Global Outlaws*, pp. 115, 118.

27   Dan Smith, *The State of the Middle East* (Berkeley: University of California Press, 2006), p. 47.

28   Christopher Parker and Pete W. Moore, "The War Economy of Iraq," *Middle East Report* 243 (Summer 2007), http://merip.org/mer/mer243/parker_moore.html, accessed October 15, 2008.

29   Much of the remainder of this section appeared in Ahmed Kanna, "Locality-in-Mobility in an Arabo-Indian Ocean City: Transnational Connections, Neoliberal Geographies, and the Production of Identity in Dubai," Anthropology Department Colloquium Presentation, University of California at Santa Cruz, January 14, 2008.

30   H. Evans, "A Note on the Wealth of Dubai," British Foreign Office Document 371/82047, June 24, 1950; K. Fenelon, *The United Arab Emirates: An Economic and Social Survey* (New York: Longman, 1976), pp. 60–65; J. Lorimer, *Gazetteer of the Persian Gulf, Oman, and Central Arabia* 2 (Amersham, UK: Demand Editions, 1984 [1915]), pp. 455–456.

31   Evans, "A Note on the Wealth of Dubai."

32   Lorimer, *Gazetteer*, pp. 455–456.

33   James Onley, "De Perse, d'Inde et d'Afrique," *Qantara* 64 (July 2007), p. 36.

34   For a discussion of how memories of urban life and alternative mappings of the city serve as mnemonics for different sociopolitical orders, see Smriti Srinivas, *Landscapes of Urban Memory: The Sacred and the Civic in India's High-Tech City* (Minneapolis: University of Minnesota Press, 2001).

35   The terms "simplifications" and "legibility" are James Scott's in *Seeing Like a State*.

36   This paragraph is taken from Kanna, "Locality-in-Mobility."

37   For a more detailed account of India–Dubai connections, see Vora, *"Impossible Citizens."*

MARYAM MONALISA GHARAVI

10

"EVERYTHING YOU CAN IMAGINE IS REAL": LABOR, HYPE, AND THE SPECTER OF PROGRESS IN DUBAI

The city is split in two. In the opulent interiors of skyscrapers far above the plebeian imagination live the masters in an idyll of technological promise. Beneath this virtual pleasure garden lies the worker's city, where drudgery takes place in a gray and dank environment. "It was their hands that built this city of ours, father," one privileged son declares. "But where do the hands belong in your scheme?"

This is the fictional city of Fritz Lang's *Metropolis*, which in 1927 created an imagined city of the future, where "those who had conceived the Tower [of Babel] did not concern themselves with the workers who built it."[2] Using a trip to New York as one of his visual and emotional inspirations, Lang commented, "I saw the buildings like a vertical curtain, opalescent, and very light. Filling the back of the stage, hanging from a sinister sky, in order to dazzle, to diffuse, to hypnotize."[3]

In *Metropolis*'s rendering of the overpowering corporate state, and the film's central narrative entanglement between wealthy owners/designers and disenfranchised workers/builders, one senses a similarity to Dubai. There is a fundamental and underemphasized tension between the visual and spatial power conveyed through Dubai's steroidal urban planning program, the might of its rulers, and the "hands" that build the city. State actors as well as journalists, geographers, developers, architects, and designers have positioned Dubai's gargantuan urbanization program within the discourse of development, renewal, modernization, "greening," and beautification. But there is an unwritten relationship between the development of Dubai for middle- and upper-class citizens and wealthy foreigners and the building of Dubai by the disenfranchised masses of mostly South Asian construction laborers. If economic figures are a relevant indication, two 2006 Mercer studies on "Cost of Living" and "Quality of Life" present an urban paradox: Dubai is prominent among the most expensive cities in which to live—it ranked 25th in March 2006, up from 73rd place in March 2005—but does not appear in the worldwide ranking of cities with the highest "quality of life."[4]

This process of marketing the space of Dubai deserves greater scrutiny. Most popular images of Dubai—at least those common in the United States and Europe—convey a lavish, exotic getaway, a "world city." From its megamalls and hyper-

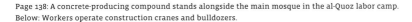

Page 138: A concrete-producing compound stands alongside the main mosque in the al-Quoz labor camp.
Below: Workers operate construction cranes and bulldozers.

markets to its mushrooming gated communities, there are enough familiar cultural indexes to make it a sought-after destination by international tourists. The media outlets of the Gulf intensify the process of branding Dubai through well-placed marketing in the guise of news articles. Regional newspapers carry headlines such as "Dubai and Abu Dhabi Win Greening and Beautification of Arab Towns" and "Launch of Spectacular New Waterfront Project 'The Lagoons' on the Dubai Creek," reflecting the news media's advocacy for state–corporate projects. The billboards that line the main city highways evoke urban fantasy. The title of this essay, "Everything You Can Imagine Is Real," is a slogan on a prominent billboard in Dubai, which the advertisers appropriated from a saying by Pablo Picasso. It evokes a beguiling city of the near-future. Such slogans are fairly conventional in their content and strategy. In their scale and skewing of temporality, however, they represent the desire to construct an entire world within the city.

How does the "world city" attract attention at the expense of the invisible laborer population? I began to examine how retail, tourist, and business space was made spectacular in Dubai, while the space of labor became a non-place. My project, consisting of film/video footage and photographs, focused on how exploitation of migrant workers underpins Dubai's self-defined urban practice as "progress."

Described as a "backwater desert state [transforming itself] into a bustling metropolis with a futuristic skyline," Dubai has some of the weakest labor regulations among rapidly industrializing countries.[5] No laws secure universal suffrage; only the *muwatinun*, or permanent citizens, are allowed to vote and retain any other civil rights. The ruler, Sheikh Muhammad bin Rashid, is the unelected leader and official arbiter of tight state–corporate control. The government considers the formation of unions a crime, forbids temporary workers to hold jobs outside their sponsorship, and resists

Labor compounds for construction workers along the main road in al-Quoz, identified only by letter, here Blocks C and D.

standardized regulation of workers' wages, sanitation, job safety, and social or medical care. It is common for workers to go unpaid for months or even years at a time.

To comprehend how urban development and labor commodification inflect each other, one must consider demographic makeup. Only about 20 percent of the approximately 4.2 million UAE residents are Emarati nationals. The disproportion in Dubai is even more pronounced. Ninety-five percent of the United Arab Emirates' workforce in the private sector is made up of migrant workers, on whom the country's economy depends. Statistical data on the countries of origin for workers are still lacking. The vast majority of laborers under the auspices of Dubai's "temporary guest worker" program come from the South Asian subcontinental rim, seeking sponsors, or *kufala'* (sing. *kafil*) in a largely informal work sector.

Of the 5,938 construction companies operating in Dubai in 2005, 76 percent were small companies employing fewer than 20 workers.[6] Migrant construction laborers, exclusively men, typically make between $1.40 to $4.00 a day,[7] and live in overcrowded work camps on the city fringes; the camps remain out of sight of five- (and now seven-) star hotels and resorts, which bring about 5 million tourists the world over to Dubai

Signs for manufacturing and servicing plants near labor compounds, al-Quoz.

each year. But one does not have to stray too far to see laborers working even in the intense summer heat. Men work off the byways of main roads, around crowded shipping docks, under the immense beams of construction passageways. In their worn clothing and head wraps, men haul concrete boulders, dig deep trenches, and move shipping freight even in heat well over 100 degrees Fahrenheit and humidity levels over 90 percent. Despite the government's claims of having restricted daytime working hours during summer, construction laborers continue to work long, blistering hours without adequate protective gear amid heat-trapping metal.

My visual research project centered on Al Quoz, one of the most dense industrial districts in Dubai. The workers' shacks are perilously stacked along Al Quoz's unlit, rubble-paved alleys. The camps that house the temporary workers consist of many rows of crude, hastily built cement-block dwellings. Men have used the panels of windows—with thick iron bars as in prison cells—as makeshift balconies to drape graying and threadbare clothing. Most advertisements for labor accommodations cater to the demands of small companies, who are given the option of housing six to eight men in 10' by 18' rooms (50 to 200 rooms per compound). Typical at many "housing complexes"— informally called ghettos—as many as twelve men share tiny, low-ceilinged rooms with bunk beds where they eat, sleep, and use the bathroom in the same confined space.

When I visited one of these blocks, typically leased to contractors or corporations at AED 3,000 (approximately $815) per room per month, I found it only half-built. The lease manager explained that his properties were speculated on, bought, and constructed at "lightning speed," and the unit would be finished within the month. When I asked how safety measures such as fire escapes, ventilation, and even the possibility of opening a window from inside the shacks would be taken into account at such a fast pace of building, he remained silent. Work camps are often the site of accidents owing to unsafe housing conditions and erratic power or water supplies in torridly hot temperatures,

A concrete factory in al-Quoz facing the labor compounds.

and cases of death by dehydration and suffocation are not uncommon. An article in the usually self-censoring UAE press of August 20, 2006, stiffly critiqued living conditions in a Deira work camp, describing it as the "The Hot House," where "hundreds shared a cramped house, and when the aircon breaks down, dozens sleep on villa's roof."[8] Antonia Carver captures these conditions well when she notes the contrast between "the messy, raw process of building a five-star hotel on $100-a-month wages and the buffed exclusivity of the end result."[9]

Just who are the workers? Figures from the Consulate General of India in Dubai show that 60 percent of the 1.2 million (majority-Keralite) Indian residents in the UAE are low-wage laborers who live in camps.[10] Other important labor-exporting countries include Pakistan, Sri Lanka, Bangladesh, and Indonesia. Chinese workers also shuttle between labor and camp sites. What unites foreign workers, aside from their hopes to remit payments to their families, is that most are forced to relinquish their passports upon entry in the UAE and at some point have their salaries illegally withheld. Workers often express despair after experiencing life in the labor camps and work-sites of Dubai, and cases of suicide by unpaid workers are common.[11]

Workers have recounted to human rights observers tales of false promises made by foreign employment agencies; mounting debts owed to labor recruiters and employers; dehydration experienced working in extreme summertime heat and humidity; industrial accidents; and depressing, desolate labor camps.[12] The Indian Embassy's official list of functions includes "processing applications received for providing free air tickets by Air India/Indian Airlines for transportation of dead bodies of destitute/stranded/absconded Indian nationals."[13]

Nearly all foreign workers travel alone, leaving families behind. The impact on the families of migrant workers is insufficiently studied, but anecdotal and limited empirical evidence is suggestive. As more men with limited social mobility leave their countries, a new syndrome has been coined in Hindi and Urdu: "Dubai chalo" ("let's go to Dubai"), which manifests itself as "disorientation [and] appears to result from social

Left: Constructing staff accommodations for Hilton Dubai Creek workers in al-Quoz.
Right: Housing up to eight men per small room, one of many advertised "deluxe labor compounds" in al-Quoz, under construction.

isolation, culture shock, harsh working conditions, and the sudden acquisition of relative wealth. Men often feel isolated and guilty for leaving their families, and the resultant sociopsychological stress can be considerable."[14] As Petra Weyland's ethnographic research on Egyptian peasant migrants to the UAE has shown, women often gather the necessary funds to support migration, and male out-migration means that wives, mothers, daughters, and sisters who stay behind carry the weight of the duties both inside and outside the home. Weyland's fieldwork points to the importance of the family and household as "the basic unit of analysis rather than the individual (migrant)."[15]

Given the markedly subordinate civil and political status of migrant workers in the Arabian Gulf, they have traditionally "opted to accommodate (to their situation) instead of entering into conflict situations, particularly with the locals."[16] This is starting to change. In recent years there have been unprecedented confrontations between construction workers and locals at both the government and street level, as well as successful attempts at increasing visibility to tourists, who are generally sheltered from ghettoes such as Al Quoz. Despite the power arrayed against them, these worker-led protests are amalgamating into a nascent but crucial movement. Headline stories on labor protests are beginning to appear on the front pages of UAE newspapers. This increased reporting, along with coverage by human rights NGOs, is increasingly seen by workers and their allies as fundamental to changing the status quo. In such ways workers challenge the prevailing discourse of Dubai urbanism, once controlled by an elite of state, sponsors, construction companies, and developers. Something like what Henri Lefebvre calls "the right to the city" is beginning to be asserted.

The growth of EMAAR Properties, among the world's largest real estate developers and one of the main entities that employ large numbers of workers, appears unstoppable. The company's net profits grew by 35 percent between the end of 2005 and the end of 2006, an increase from almost $1.29 billion to almost $1.74 billion.[17] By the end of 2007, the company was reporting net annual profits of approximately $1.81 billion. Annual revenue for 2007 was 25 percent higher than that for 2006. As the chairman of EMAAR, Muhammad al-Abbar, commented about 2007: "In a tough year for the global property market, EMAAR recorded impressive financials, testament to the strong fundamentals that drive the company." According to Ahmed Abdel Rahman, a financial analyst for Amana Capital, "The results for 2007 came in line with expectations. The increase ... (in net profits) is the same level achieved during the past few years." "Earnings of EMAAR Properties during the fourth quarter (of 2007)," he added, "were the highest in the company's history." Also in 2007, *The Financial Times* gave its imprimatur to the company, nominating it to the newspaper's "Global 500 List."[18]

In 2006, nearly 20,000 workers filed complaints with the government protesting unpaid wages and intolerable living conditions.[19] In March 2006, workers at EMAAR's Burj Dubai staged an ambitious strike. Nearly 2,500 workers demanded better work conditions and increased pay. The week-long dispute highlighted the exploitive economic strategies of megaproject developers (who pay no taxes) and the state that supports them. As Antonia Carver has put it, the companies exploit "the very bottom rung of the property ladder" to maximize profits and reduce their reliance on huge loans.[20]

Henri Lefebvre argues that space is never "an indifferent medium, the sum of places where surplus value is created, realized, and distributed." Rather, it is the "product of social labor, the very general object of production, and consequently of the formation of surplus value [...] within the very framework of neocapitalism."[21] As Khalaf and Alkobaisi have shown, "were we to pull away the global constituents of the migrants' ethnoscape from a society like the UAE, the entire society would cease to be what it is now, as more than 80 [percent] of its population would be eliminated. This in turn would generate severe repercussions throughout the society. The whole development process would come to a halt."[22]

Human Rights Watch, Amnesty International, Mafiwasta, and other watchdog and advocacy organizations have called for the UAE to reform its labor laws in conformity with the standards of the International Labor Organization and to become a signatory to the International Convention on the Protection of the Rights of All Migrant Workers and Members of Their Families (MWC).[23] Yet, according to observers, without extensive structural changes to enable enforcement of human and labor rights, the UAE Ministry of Labour "has neither the manpower nor the ability to adequately protect over a million unskilled migrant workers."[24]

Lefebvre identifies three distinct but coexisting epistemes: the urbanism of humanists (who propose abstract utopias); of developers (who sell urbanism, or "happiness, lifestyle, a certain social standing"); and of the state and its technocrats. All three epistemes, according Lefebvre, converge on "the modern philosophy of the city, justified by (liberal) humanism while justifying a (technocratic) utopia."[25] The flaw of this liberal philosophy of the city is its erasure of the social underpinnings of the making of urban space. Dubai manifests this convergence in its seamless connection between state executive (Sheikh Muhammad), developers and holding companies (EMAAR, Nakheel, Dubai Holding, etc.), and technocratic elite (al-Abbar, Nakheel chairman Ahmed

Buses carrying workers across construction sites run at all hours.
Almost none are air-conditioned.

bin Sulaym, and Dubai Holding chairman Muhammad al-Gergawi). This elite's vision of the urban is in turn reflected in globally circulated images of the city as a tourist destination and architectural discourses that privilege technical or prestige considerations over the social dimensions of urban life. For Lefebvre, the "the worst utopia" is that which "belongs to the state. It is a state utopia: a cloud on the mountain that blocks the road."[26] Lefebvre was aiming his critique at the developmentalist, modernist state, but his skepticism also applies to today's city, with its domination by private capital, deterritorialized cultural flows, and floating elites. Both the modernist city of Lefebvre's day and the global city of our own are characterized by the privileging of instrumental approaches over the totality of relations that produce, and are produced by, urban space. Both attempt to whitewash the real history of their production with narrow, aestheticized, locally, regionally, and globally scaled notions of "progress." Contrary to the boosterism of contemporary Dubai, the authoritarian traditions of the modernist city "weigh like a nightmare on the brain of the living."[27]

Notes

The idea for a film/video project in Dubai developed in a film course led by Lucien Taylor, as a treatment called "Empty Towers." I wish to thank him for his encouragement and support. I also thank Robb Moss for zeroing in on the obsession with progress, the undercurrent of my project and this essay. I am most indebted to Ahmed Bensouda, whose unflinching eye, empathy, and extensive field knowledge made this essay and my visual work possible.

1   Philip Watson, "Buy Buy Dubai," *The Irish Times*, March 25, 2006: 14.

2   Fritz Lang, *Metropolis,* Babelsberg Studios, 1927.

3   *Metropolis*, commentary track, Murnau Foundation DVD.

4   Mercer Human Resources Consulting, "Cost of Living Survey" and "Worldwide Quality of Living Survey," 2006. www.mercern.HR.com (accessed June 29, 2006).

5   N.A., "Labourers in UAE Struggle to Escape Poverty," *Daily Times of Pakistan*, April 11, 2005.

6   Human Rights Watch, "Building Towers, Cheating Workers: Exploitation of Migrant Construction Workers in the United Arab Emirates," November 12, 2006. http://hrw.org/reports/2006/uae1106 (accessed November 15, 2005).

7   N.A., "Dubai Labour Unrest Continues," *Al Jazeera English*, March 25, 2006. http://english.aljazeera.net/news/archive/archive?ArchiveId=19388 (accessed December 4, 2006).

8   N.A., "The Hot House," *7 Days (*UAE*)*, August 20, 2006, pp. 1–6.

9   Antonia Carver, "Cautious Radicals: Art and the Invisible Majority," *Bidoun* 7, Spring/Summer 2006, pp. 82–86.

10 Ibid.

11 "Labourers in UAE Struggle," *Daily Times*.

12 Human Rights Watch, "Building Towers, Cheating Workers."

13 Carver, "Cautious Radicals."

14 "Impact of Migration to the Persian Gulf Countries," Library of Congress Country Studies, April 1994. http://lcweb2.loc.gov/frd/cs/pktoc.html (accessed June 14, 2006).

15 Petra Weyland, "Egyptian Peasant Migrants Heading for the Gulf States: Upon the Relevance of the Household as an Analytical Category for Migration Theory," in H. Rudolph and M. Morokvasic, eds., *Bridging States and Markets: International Migration in the Early 1990s* (Berlin: Sigma, 1993), pp. 209–224.

16 Sulayman Khalaf and Saad Alkobaisi, "Migrants' Strategies of Coping and Patterns of Accommodation in the Oil-Rich Gulf Societies: Evidence from the UAE," *British Journal of Middle Eastern Studies*, 26, No. 2 (November 1999), pp. 271–298.

17 N.A., "EMAAR Profits Increase by 35 Percent," *Daily Times of Pakistan,* February 1, 2007, http://www.dailytimes.com.pk/default.asp?page=2007%5C02%5C01%5C story_1-2-2007_pg5_12 (accessed April 6, 2008).

18 The remainder of this paragraph is based on Mohamad Al Kady, "EMAAR Profits Reach Dh1.7bn in Fourth Quarter," *Emirates Business 24/7,* January 17, 2008, http://www.business24-7.ae/cs/article_show_mainh1_story.aspx?HeadlineID=1093 (accessed April 6, 2008).

19 Human Rights Watch, "Building Towers."

20 Carver, "Cautious Radicals."

21 Henri Lefebvre, *The Urban Revolution,* Robert Bononno, trans. (Minneapolis: University of Minnesota Press, 2003), p. 155.

22 Khalaf and Alkobaisi, "Migrants' Strategies," p. 274.

23 Under the auspices of the UN High Commissioner for Human Rights.

24 N.A., "Human Rights Watch Report Turns Up the Heat," November 13, 2006. http://www.mafiwasta.com (accessed November 15, 2006).

25 Lefebvre, *Urban Revolution,* p. 155.

26 Ibid., p. 163.

27 Karl Marx, "The Eighteenth Brumaire of Louis Bonaparte," in R. Tucker, ed., *Marx–Engels Reader* (New York: Norton, 1978), p. 595.

KEVIN MITCHELL

11

THE FUTURE PROMISE OF
ARCHITECTURE IN DUBAI

In a 2005 article on real-estate development in
Dubai, journalist Andrew Hammond referred to
the emirate as an "architect's paradise." Reporting
on extraordinary proposals that included full-
scale interpretations of the Tower of Babel and
the Great Pyramid of Giza, Hammond described a
place where anything appears to be possible.

According to one architect interviewed for the article, "Abroad you need to go through certain procedures and zoning rights, but here there is the momentum, speed and excitement and clients want everything up yesterday. It's very satisfying."[1] While Dubai's lack of controls may appeal to developers who wish to maximize rates of return and to architects who seek to transcend reality, it is questionable whether their efforts will result in the idyllic settings that a paradise promises.

The term "paradise" may have been more significant than Hammond realized. The original Persian root *pairidaêza* referred to a wall enclosing a garden and orchard. The word came to English via Xenophon, the well-traveled Greek who was born in the fifth century B.C. and later served in the Persian Army. In his writings, Xenophon employed the variation *paradiesos* to describe the private walled enclosures that contained the gardens of royalty. All things considered, perhaps Dubai can be described as a paradise at its most etymologically precise: the emirate's boundaries delimit a space within which a select group rely on foreign labor to turn sand into gardens and harvest the fruits of private property and exclusive commercial distribution agreements that remain concentrated in the hands of a few.

Measures to attract mercantile activity from across the region in the early twentieth century provided the foundation for a multicultural population bound together by financial interest. And adopting core neoliberal values such as liberalization of the financial sector and the free flow of foreign direct investment has encouraged extraordinary growth, especially in the real-estate sector. While Dubai has employed architecture as primary component of a comprehensive branding strategy, the momentum and speed that results from treating buildings as objects of consumption may ultimately keep the representations from becoming reality.

THE PROMISE OF ARCHITECTURE

As real-estate speculation fuels the construction industry, buildings must compete for iconic status to attract the attention of tourists and investors, which in some cases are one and the same. Photorealistic images, sometimes generated without an actual site and selected or on the basis of nothing more than a vague idea, indicate lush gardens, ample parking, and a few nondescript neighboring structures to ensure incredible views and privacy. However, the realities that must be confronted in the design and construction processes make it difficult to deliver on the promises inherent in sales brochures and billboards.

The myopic focus on individual buildings at the expense of cohesive urban plans have implications for both singular works of architecture and the urban environment; in the words of Nick Tosches in *Vanity Fair*, "It is the visual equivalent of a bunch of speed freaks babbling incoherently to one another."[2] Tosches, like many others, cannot resist comparisons between Dubai and Las Vegas. Although the planned "Bawadi" development includes a 10-kilometer entertainment corridor that seeks to rival the Las Vegas Strip, the connections between Dubai and what Alistair Cooke described as "Everyman's cut-rate Babylon" are often superficial and tend to be limited to the themed

Page 148: Recreation through re-creation
Above: Promises

developments. However, more significant similarities resulting from rapid growth war-rant consideration, as these may ultimately affect long-term prospects in Dubai.

Both Las Vegas and Dubai are transient cities that rely on a constant flow of visi-tors and low-wage labor for construction and service industries. However, there are significant differences, as approximately 70 percent of hotel and restaurant workers in Las Vegas are members of unions and, as concluded by the authors of "The Coffee Pot Wars: Union and Firm Restructuring of the Hotel Industry," average hourly wages in the hotel industry are higher among non-union members in cities where organized labor exists.[3] While no official statistics for Dubai's service industries are publicly avail-able, reports and classified job advertisements indicate that offers of employment and wages are sometimes determined by gender and nationality rather than qualification. The disparities that exist in the construction industry in Dubai seem even greater. Although "legal" non-union workers who support the building boom in Las Vegas should be guaranteed a minimum wage and safety protection under U.S. Occupational Safety and Health Administration (OSHA) regulations, the welfare of laborers in the UAE is not protected by comparable legislation or consistent enforcement. And while labor unrest has brought attention to the conditions endured by those actually responsible for building high-profile property development projects in Dubai, it is unclear whether comprehensive measures will be implemented to address the situation.

One of the major challenges is the regulation of private firms operating in Dubai. In a candid newspaper interview in 2006, the head of the Inspection Department of the UAE Ministry of Labor lamented the shortage of inspectors that prohibited ensuring compliance with labor laws at construction sites. According to the article, twenty inspectors were responsible for monitoring 70,000 construction sites in addition to the accommodation for laborers. The official stated: "In my opinion we need hundreds of new inspectors to cope with the fast growing number of building sites and the accommodation for labourers. We are currently finding it difficult to cope."[4] Low salaries, hazardous conditions, and long working hours make recruitment of inspectors difficult and, according to the official, the severe shortage makes it possible for any laws that exist to be continually ignored. While cursory regulatory policies for governing the construction industry have been announced, implementation and consistent enforcement remains an issue (as discussed earlier in this volume).

In September 2006, the *Gulf News* quoted a UAE Ministry of Labor official who indicated that a mandatory two-day weekend was being contemplated for the private sector, but that a minimum wage would not be considered.[5] However, even if measures for two-day weekends and a minimum wage are adopted, it is unlikely that they can be adequately followed up and enforced in sectors in which delays affect return on investment. As addressed in greater detail below, the limited regulation and lack of enforcement in the construction industry affects not only the individual worker but can also influence the general level of quality achieved in buildings.

Rapid growth in both Las Vegas and Dubai has resulted in a disparity between the populations and the necessary infrastructure: roads, schools, and supplies of water and electricity cannot keep pace with the rapid increases in demand. While Dubai is investing heavily in public transportation initiatives to address severe traffic congestion, viability may ultimately depend on incentives that decrease dependence on the automobile and policies that reward or encourage use. Inexpensive fuel, low import duties, and an informal network of resale among low-wage earners contribute to widespread car ownership. According to the Dubai Municipality's statistics, the total number of vehicles registered in the emirate in 2002 was 306,312; by 2005, the number had risen to 487,903.[6] While the increase was substantial, conflicting data released by the municipality indicates that the figure for 2005 may have been too low, citing that a total of 621,278 vehicles were registered during the year.[7] If this figure is correct, then the number of vehicles in Dubai doubled within three years. Given the sheer number of vehicles and the decentralization into a myriad of business/residential enclaves, it will be a challenge to deal with the issue of traffic and decrease dependence on automobiles in a city that has been designed around them.

Located in arid regions, Las Vegas and Dubai also both face real challenges with providing sufficient water supplies: The Rocky Mountain Institute has reported that Las Vegas has one of the highest rates of water consumption per capita in the United States;[8] and an Emirates Industrial Bank study concluded that the UAE has one of the highest water consumption levels in the world.[9] In spite of excessive consumption and damage to aquifers resulting from groundwater extraction, indigenous plants that are well suited to the climatic conditions in the UAE have been shunned in favor of "beautification" schemes that include extensive manicured lawns in unlikely places—for example, in traffic interchanges or medians.

Data from the Dubai Municipality indicates that the total amount of "green area" in the emirate was 3,486,202 square meters at the end of 1997;[10] by the end of 2005, the "green area" had nearly doubled to 6,748,066 square meters.[11] Although desalinated water is often used for irrigation, treating seawater, brackish water, or wastewater is energy intensive. The World Resources Institute reports that in 1997 the energy consumption per capita for the United States and the UAE was, respectively, 7.96 and 13.38 (in thousand of metric tons of oil equivalent). As a point of comparison, in the same year the energy consumption per capita in the entire Middle East and North Africa region was 1.39.[12] The *United Arab Emirates Country Report* issued by the The Economist Intelligence Unit notes that infrastructure development poses a risk to the real estate market in Dubai: "Providing water, power and sewerage to all of the new developments is a challenging task, and some developers have privately voiced concerns that proposed demand may exceed proposed supply."[13]

Superficial comparisons limited to themed tourist destinations only serve to obscure the more startling similarities between Dubai and Las Vegas. Although both cities suffer from some of the same effects of rapid urbanization, the causes of growth are quite different. Relaxed gaming laws have supported the transformation of Las Vegas into an entertainment center, while Dubai has relied on its location and long-standing position as a trade hub. With limited oil reserves, diversification to move away from the rentier economies of some of its neighbors has become increasingly important.

Dubai has achieved economic success resulting from importing and reexporting activities, and there has been an increasing focus on attracting foreign direct investment in the real-estate sector since the 1990s. According to the International Monetary Fund (IMF), "The pace of liberalization gained momentum, in particular in Dubai, and to a lesser extent in the other Emirates. Dubai's policy of extending foreign ownership of land and properties for real estate developments have resulted in a construction boom and a significant increase in FDI in this sector."[14]

When searching for precedents to assist in understanding Dubai's uncanny ability to attract real-estate investment, one can look at cases where architecture has been successfully employed as a marketing tool to sell a city not yet built. One such example is the building boom that took place in Sarasota, Florida, in the mid-1920s. In "Selling Sarasota: Architecture and Propaganda in a 1920s Boom Town," Michael McDonough points out that the number of real-estate firms had increased from 15 in 1924 to more than 200 in 1926.[15] A Dubai Chamber of Commerce and Industry (DCCI) report from 2000 states: "Last year there were about 500 licenses to real estate firms and this, according to specialists, is more than the needs of the market."[16] A follow-up study noted that there were 938 active "enterprises" working within the real-estate sector in 2003; it was also reported that "With regards of the age distribution of the real estate enterprises, almost 50% of the active enterprises included in the DCCI database are 4 years old or less. The enterprises of ages between 5 and 9 years are 30% while 12% are 10 to 14 years old."[17] IMF data reveals that the number of employees in real estate in the UAE nearly doubled from 42,000 in 2000 to an estimated 81,000 in 2005.[18]

Beautification

Like Dubai, Sarasota benefited from an undeveloped coastline and a seemingly endless supply of speculative developers. McDonough cites an article from a 1926 issue of *Harper's Monthly Magazine* that describes the situation in clear terms: "The smell of money in Florida, which attracts men as the smell of blood attracts a wild animal, became ripe and strong last spring. The whole United States began to catch whiffs of it. Pungent tales of immense wealth carried far."[19] The similarities between Sarasota and Dubai do not end with waterfront property and the ability to attract wealth; those driving development in both places have relied on fanciful renderings and what McDonough describes as "carefully contrived site tours" to attract buyers. Whereas Sarasota relied on the promotional acumen of circus mogul John Ringling, Dubai's public/private corporations spare no expense when it comes to marketing in the form of corporate sponsorships and spectacular real-estate initiatives intended to attract media attention. However, while Sarasota was to be developed according to John Nolen's comprehensive development plan that sought to transform the town into pseudo-Mediterranean resort, Dubai consists of numerous small enclaves that are marketed as "cities" or "villages"—each with varying degrees of coherence.

The Dubai Waterfront development, promised to be larger than Manhattan and Beirut, is described as "an unprecedented 81 million metres-squared mixed-use land-mark development without equal .... [that] will feature well over 100 different waterfront developments and over 150 master planned communities and investment opportunities."[20] According to the branding consultants, the developer "challenged us with branding a project years from completion, one that needed to generate billions of dollars from investors."[21] And examples such as the Palm Islands are clearly conscious attempts to generate publicity: "If there was no Burj Dubai, no Palm, no World, would anyone be speaking of Dubai today?...You shouldn't look at projects as crazy stand-alones. It's part of building the brand."[22] In keeping with the emphasis on exaggeration that characterizes other Dubai developments, the Palm Islands have gained much from being visible from orbiting satellites. And visitors to the developer's website are told that the planned "Palm Diera" will have the distinction of being the biggest of the "trilogy" of three planned palm-shaped land forms and the largest man-made island in the world. Although the "Palm Jumeirah" and the "Palm Jebel Ali" are being constructed outside of Dubai's core, the "Palm Diera" will extend Dubai's most urbanized district into the Gulf. The promotional literature for the "Palm Diera" proposal developed by the planning consultants speaks of advanced transit systems, creating comfortable walkable places, efficient infrastructure, and energy conservation using natural cooling and light. This seems incongruent with the developer's sales pitch, except for the rhetoric of New Urbanism that refers to rather vague notions of "community." The planner's description mentions a "new cosmopolitan community," and the developer's website states that the first residents of the "Palm Jumeirah" will form "the core of a community that will encompass more than seventy nationalities."[23]

Given the diverse nature of the population in Dubai, the extreme socioeconomic distinctions that exist, and the absence of conditions that facilitate the development of an inclusive civil society or public sphere, marketing material that employs terms such

White elephants in the media circus

as "community" seems naive. Rather than fundamentally addressing the conditions that exist, architecture and urban design risks becoming reduced to providing surface-level decoration that is devoid of broader significance. In an article entitled "Paradise Planned: Community Formation and the Master Planned Estate," Gabrielle Gwyther argued that a necessary precondition for success is a "community compact," defined as "a broad agreement between the planner-developer and the residents as to the primary development goal and the dominant value system or common social code which is intended to operate within the estate."[24] Using case studies of two master-planned housing estates in Sydney, Gwyther examined the relationships between economic interests and community association using the concept of social capital, which is based on the notion that individuals invest in social relations with expected returns. For example, all residents behave in a similar manner, and respect covenants and other restrictions; in return the development is promoted as a desirable place to live and is distinguished from other neighborhoods. While the study supported the claim that the community compact can potentially intensify homogeneity among residents, it should be noted that demographic data cited in the article reveal that residents of the two housing estates shared many characteristics: 77.2–82.5 percent were born in Australia; 92.6–93.3 percent spoke only English; 80.2–81.4 percent were Christian; and there was a limited range of educational levels and occupations. Applied to the UAE, Gwyther's model is challenged as a result of the fundamental requirement for a common social code or dominant value system. Of the estimated 80 percent of the population that are non-nationals, there is great diversity.

In an article on Gulf demography, sociologist Andrzej Kapiszewski concluded:

In all the GCC states the employment of the nationals and the labor migration will remain politically a very sensitive issue as it will cause further tensions between the profit-driven concerns of the private sector, the indigenization efforts of the states and the national security considerations. Moreover, a large number of foreigners residing in these countries will bring new social and cultural challenges of consequences difficult to estimate, especially as the naturalization of many foreigners will take place. Asians will continue to dominate the foreign workforce at the expense of the non-Gulf Arab labor.[25]

CAN PROMISES BE KEPT?

In addition to the discrepancy between visions of "community" and reality, early images of completed portions of "Palm Jumeirah" also reveal disparities between representation and reality. Most striking is the density of the large single-family homes that will occupy the fronds. Aerial renderings in promotional brochures show lush green belts with intermittent houses; however, photographs of completed projects reveal something altogether different, namely a development pattern intended to maximize available land. Gargantuan residences are squeezed into small plots; with what appears to be a zero lot line on one side and a minimum setback on the other, the distance between individual buildings is nominal. According to the developer, "Home owners will be able to watch the sunset while taking a dip in their private pool." Given the development pattern and the proximity of neighboring buildings, it is unlikely that any pool will have the desired degree of privacy. And only half of the frond inhabitants will be able to enjoy the sunset; the other half will live in residences facing east and must therefore be content with the sunrise over Dubai's expanding skyline.

Investors remain steadfast, in spite of the incongruence between rendering and reality and significant construction delays. Although the developer offered buyers the opportunity to sell back their property at the original sale price plus interest, there were reportedly no takers. This was attributed to the fact that the market price for the properties has more than doubled since the original purchase. However, other buyers in less prestigious projects have been less fortunate. In October 2006, the *Malaysia Sun* newspaper reported that the Marina Quays, a residential project being developed by in the Dubai Marina, had yet to begin construction, although some units were purchased over two years prior. Buyers complained that the developer benefits from the interest on the purchase price while they are charged 10.6 percent per annum on late installments.

Unbridled developments that seek to maximize profit make it impossible for developers and their architects to deliver on the "promises" implied in sales brochures; the rapid increase in property values and the possibility of resale before completion fuels speculation. Short-term profits will not be affected as property is purchased prior to construction with small deposits and "flipped" (i.e., almost immediately resold to the next investor). Given the fact that the first wave of Dubai's high-profile developments remains unfinished, it is not possible to predict what the implications will be when projects are occupied. But hints do appear as apartments nearing completion are posted for sale via the websites of real-estate brokers offering "offshore investments." The last in line are now beginning to see what they have purchased: buildings presented as standing alone on an expansive lawn have been surrounded by even taller buildings that threaten privacy; apartments with the promise of a "marina view" are left with only a glimpse of sea, sky, and an aluminum plant. View corridors and fundamental urban design principles intended to balance the interests of individual building owners with master plans quickly disintegrate when confronted with liberal economic forces unrestrained by comprehensive urban design strategies and legislation that governs implementation.

The lack of comprehensive urban design strategies may affect not only infrastructure but also investor confidence over the long term as the limits of influence of property owners become clearer. One such example is known as the "Parallel Roads Project." Intended to ease congestion caused by rush-hour commuters, the road will cut through residential areas, including the upscale development known as "Emirates Hills." When freehold owners purchased property, there were no plans for main arteries to run through the area; however, population increases and heavier traffic loads demanded alternatives. While Dubai openly publicizes its goal to dramatically increase the emirate's population, the almost constant infrastructure improvements seem to address only existing conditions rather than long-term projections. Current freehold legislation

From rendering to reality

remains vague and seems to grant nothing more than residency; therefore property owners have no recourse through public agencies. When asked about the concerns raised by residents that would potentially be affected by the roads project, the Chairman of Dubai's Road and Transport Authority (RTA) stated: "We understand their concerns and we will arrange a meeting with them soon to discuss the project. We want to give them the right information and to invite them to make suggestions. But we will not be changing the plans."[26] This reiterated an earlier statement indicating that plans were final and encouraging residents to leave their recommendations in a suggestion box.

Do architects themselves have any more say than the freehold property owners invited to make suggestions on plans already finalized? Andrew Hammond notes in his article that some leading British architects that are at work in Dubai have "slammed the building frenzy in high-profile journals, rueing the lack of vernacular tradition to influence the stylistic direction."[27] In an article from February 15, 2005, the *Gulf News* reported that indeed "One of Britan's most renowned architects had labeled new buildings springing up in Dubai as "terrible."[28] For Dubai observers, this frank assessment of the quality of some recent buildings was both surprising and welcome. There was hope that the comments indicated the arrival of a critical debate focused on the built environment. This was not to be. Two days later, the same newspaper published a retraction in the form of an article entitled "Britan's top architect lauds building designs in Dubai."[29] Within a matter of days, the state of architecture in the emirate seemed to have improved dramatically, as did the status of the architect as he was elevated from one of Britan's "most renowned" to the "top architect."

Although much of the criticism directed at the state of architecture in Dubai has been well founded, the individual building remains a vital aspect of marketing and promotional campaigns. Given the importance placed on singular buildings in marketing, one would expect an emphasis on quality of design and construction. But, as noted above, initial investors have often sold property well before construction begins, and it is likely that the property has been "flipped" before it reaches the owner who will possess the title at the time of completion. The fact that the initial investors who may have commissioned the project have no vested interest in the completed work, the demand for speed in design and construction processes, the harsh natural environment, and the general skill level in an imported and low-wage workforce adversely affect architecture in Dubai. While real-estate speculation and its resultant problems are widespread and by no means specific to the UAE, the convergence of forces mentioned above result from the particular situation found there.

A "rush job" is how Frank Gehry referred to the four-month deadline for the design for the Guggenheim franchise planned for Abu Dhabi.[30] It is not surprising that four months for the design of a major museum would be viewed as rushed; however, given that this is a project deemed to be of importance, it is astonishing that the architect was given sixteen weeks and that the announcement came without an "artist's rendering" of the project. The speed with which projects move from announcement to the start of construction in the UAE is as astonishing as the accelerated building schedules. Proposed projects are usually closely guarded and announced with great fanfare, large models, and fanciful renderings. The fact that Gehry was given four months after the official announcement is actually an indicator of negotiating power.

The accelerated pace of development devalues architecture. Thorough processes of design and planning require time and the benefits tend to be long term. Foundations for fast-track projects are poured before designs are complete and, in some cases, perhaps even before the design development phase begins. Of course this has implications for the quality of architecture. Even on the surface, it is possible to see the effects that this has had—hastily completed projects exhibit unresolved details and show signs of wear after a very short time. As projects are completed and buyers are beginning inspections, the internet has provided an unexpected venue for individual owners who have purchased property to voice concerns about construction quality. The forum section at Skyscrapercity.com has devoted a section of the site to the UAE and it is being used to track progress of construction, air grievances, and serve as an incubator for organizing homeowners groups, in some cases even before construction has begun. Buyers exchange information and post responses they have received from developers. In addition to myriad complaints related to completion delays, owners post inspection photographs that reveal poor workmanship.

Substandard construction practices could have significant long-term repercussions related to the maintenance and care of buildings. According to an article in the GCC edition of *Facilities Management Magazine*:

> Many developers and landowners in the Gulf region do not consider the full facility life cycle cost. Instead, prominence is given to the pre-sales of units and managing the profit margins between construction costs and the initial pre-sales values. Therefore, on numerous occasions the equation between squeezing the lowest possible construction cost and the total lifetime cost of a facility is not properly balanced.[31]

According to the authors, the total value of construction projects is $176 billion (excluding oil and gas projects). Over a twenty-five-year period, it is estimated that the life-cycle costs for these projects will be $704 billion. One could expect that these costs could rise with the increased demands resulting from the harsh climate and quality of workmanship and materials used in speculative developments. As noted earlier, if the real-estate market continues to perform well, then initial investments that are quickly "flipped" will likely result in a high rate of return; however, long-term owners find that costs associated with maintenance and repair may require much more attention than initially expected.

Although the quality of design and construction for major projects was higher in the Arabian Gulf during the first wave of development following the discovery of oil, there were also significant obstacles. In a 1976 issue of the *Bulletin for the British Society for Middle Eastern Studies*, Christopher Mitchell reported: "The challenges to an architect working within such a milieu are many and varied. Perhaps the simplest— though nonetheless important—are the technical constructional problems (relating to ground conditions and standards and availability of materials), and the need to use building forms and detailing to minimize the effects of the extreme climate experienced."[32] Mitchell's pragmatic but nonetheless insightful observations in the three-page report still resonate thirty years on.

In spite of the harsh climate in the UAE, few developers insist on measures that would reduce long-term monetary and environmental costs associated with excessive energy consumption. Given the subsidies that exist, there are no incentives and no need to consider the short-term costs that would result from taking steps to invest time in the design of passive cooling strategies or money in more efficient active systems. Although official statistics from Dubai are difficult to acquire, an Industry Canada website reports that the cost of generating one kW hour of electricity in Abu Dhabi is seven cents; the selling price is four cents to non-UAE nationals and commercial offices and two cents to UAE nationals.[33] There have been discussions of discontinuing subsidies and, should this happen, demands may be made by purchasers and end-users. However, given that the majority of residents are part of the expatriate labor force who move to the UAE for the short to medium term, the cost may be passed on to tenants who will have little say in design-related strategies that could reduce consumption while maintaining comfort during periods of extreme heat.

The concerns that Mitchell voiced in 1976 regarding building materials seem to remain. A report entitled "Steel Quality Fears Grow as Costs Rise" outlined the potential problems associated with using inferior quality steel for components such as steel reinforcing bars for concrete structures. Given cost increases and material shortages, it seems that substandard and fake steel building products are now flooding the market in the UAE and neighboring GCC countries. The Dubai Municipality recognized this problem and carried out random tests using samples from government projects. Out of 250 samples, 99 percent were reported to have complied with the minimum standards. However, no private projects were subject to testing. According to an anonymous product tester, "Some customers are very clever.... Whenever they have a product that is sub-standard they will not test it. Everyone is looking for a cheaper option—that's the problem."[34]

Although the UAE has a small manufacturing base that produces building materials, supplies cannot keep pace with demand. Costs have therefore increased and data from 2005 indicated an annual increase of 21 percent for a bag of cement and 25 percent for ready-mix concrete.[35] There is also the issue of quality and the potential discrepancy between price level and the ultimate worth of the completed building. High humidity, extreme temperatures, and high salt content in subsoils continue to present challenges to the construction industry in the UAE. Speaking at a conference on concrete technology, an industry expert indicated that the service life of reinforced concrete is significantly lower in the UAE than in other parts of the world and that there is a tendency to use a "trial-and-error" approach to materials and processes that have not been standardized or fully tested. The ultimate conclusion was that "in this market, if something is difficult to do, they simply tend not to do it."[36]

Some of the difficulties were attributed to an expatriate workforce with varying levels of knowledge, training, and experience. This is not surprising given the process of recruiting and retaining construction workers. The general plight of low-wage earners and the reasons for the lack of enforcement of basic labor laws have been mentioned above, and the situation in the construction industry seems to be severe. With regard to experience or qualification, few of the low-wage workers seem prepared for work in the construction industry, especially in trades such as finish carpentry. In a study of workers from the Indian state of Kerala, John Willoughby indicates that two-thirds have no higher or technical training.[37] Even among those that have been trained as carpenters or technicians, it is questionable whether their skills match the demands that would seem to be required for multimillion-dollar residential projects where expectations are high and careful attention to detail is required. While the construction industry pays premiums for design and managerial expertise, those responsible for execution are expected to deliver exceptional work in spite of substandard conditions and compensation.

Dubai has successfully attracted what John Urry has termed "the tourist gaze," with buildings characterized by novelty rather than innovation.[38] The short-term gains in the form of high hotel occupancy rates will certainly have long-term environmental consequences that are already attracting attention. The UAE continues to have the greatest "ecological footprint" (per person) in the world, according to the World Wide Fund for Nature (WWF). This has been calculated as the demand in terms of the area of biologically productive land and sea required to provide the necessary resources and absorb the waste that is produced. According to the WWF *Living Planet Report* 2004, the global ecological footprint was 2.2 global hectares per person; the ecological footprint for the UAE was reported to be the highest at 9.9.[39] The global ecological footprint remained the same in the WWF Living Planet Report 2006;[40] however, the UAE increased to 11.9, once again the highest published in the report. The majority of the ecological footprint resulted from carbon dioxide from fossil fuels, and the UAE led the world in this category. While the petrochemical and metals industries contribute to the high energy consumption, it has been estimated that during the summer season 75–85 percent of the total power generated is used for air conditioning;[41] and cooling can cost owners of high-rises as much as 30 percent of the total cost of the building over the life of the structure.[42]

All of the factors mentioned above conspire against the individual work of architecture and increase the challenges associated with producing buildings that are of lasting value. In an essay entitled "Less for Less Yet: On Architecture's Value(s) in the Marketplace," Michael Benedikt stated:

> Architecture, as an industry, broadly conceived, has become less and less able to deliver a superior, evolving and popularly engaging product that can compete with other, more successful products–with cars, music, movies, sports, and travel, to name a few. And the less successfully architecture has competed with these diverse "growth industries," the less architects have been entrusted with the time and money to perform work on a scale and with a quality that could perhaps, turn things around.[43]

Benedikt rightly notes both time and money are required for quality. Relaxed real-estate laws, liberal banking regulations, and high oil prices result in a seemingly endless flow of capital that settles in Dubai. However, as the demand to see immediate return on investment increases, there is a decrease in the time allowed for design, planning, and construction.

CONCLUSION

Dubai has benefitted from embracing core neoliberal values such as liberalization of the financial sector, the free flow of foreign direct investment, privatization of service sectors, and liberal trade policies. The measures taken to attract mercantile activity from across the region in the early twentieth century provided the foundation for a multicultural population bound together by the pursuit of profit. Just as early traders fled to Dubai to escape increases in taxes, investors are now attracted by relaxed legislation and returns generated by profit margins resulting from a seemingly endless supply of low-wage labor.

The United Nations Conference on Trade and Development's (UNCTD) *World Investment Report 2006* notes liberalization in the areas of electricity and water in the UAE and the fact that the country received $12 billion in foreign direct investment in 2005, the largest inflow in West Asia. As noted in the report, real- estate investment has made a significant contribution: "Driven by property laws enacted successively in Abu Dhabi and Dubai, FDI in real estate is likely to remain prominent."[44] If this prediction is correct, then the construction industry may continue to benefit from foreign direct investment into new and ever-larger real-estate projects. But will this increase in quantity result in qualitative changes in the built environment?

As a result of neoliberal market forces and the demands to maximize returns on investment within the short term, the buildings and urban space tend to be treated as commodities, just like any other that passes through Dubai's efficient ports. However, unlike the goods and capital that flow through Dubai, buildings and infrastructure remain and will affect the long-term viability of the city. While for most of the residents in the UAE, the staggering statistics revealing that the Dubai-based port operator DP world has a global capacity of 50 million TEU (twenty foot equivalent unit; the standard measure of capacity in the container industry) remain abstract. But the effects of rapid urban development are much more tangible as they directly impact the quality of life in the UAE: traffic jams, water shortages, and electricity interruptions that currently represent inconveniences may intensify as population increases beyond the capacity of infrastructure.

Expertise in the areas of architecture and planning exists in Dubai. But considerable challenges remain in spite of isolated attempts at developing buildings based on innovation rather than novelty and efforts to reduce the excessive consumption of resources, thereby reducing the UAE's disproportionate "ecological footprint." As long as buildings are viewed as short- to medium-term investments, design (and its benefits that can only be realized over the longer term) will continue to be devalued. While an architect with the status of Frank Gehry can perhaps negotiate four months for the design of a major building, those who are even more affected by market forces may not be afforded that "extravagance."

Many have criticized the rapid urbanization on the basis that it has resulted in an imported architecture that is insensitive to the "culture" of the UAE. Unfortunately these critiques are often mired in nostalgia and hampered by vague notions of "traditional," "modern," and "identity"; further confusion results when claims are supported by advocating themed developments that reduce elements like the *barjeel*, or windtower, to a visual accoutrement. In *The Crisis of Culture: Its Social and Its Political Significance*, Hannah Arendt traced the term "culture" to the original Roman *colere*—to cultivate, to dwell, to take care of.[45] For Arendt, cultivation included entering into a reciprocal relationship with the natural world in order to make a space for human habitation. She further made distinctions between objects of culture and objects of consumption: cultural objects should endure and transcend their immediate use value; objects of consumption have little lasting value and are commodities to be used and discarded. In cases where foreign direct investment is translated into a speculative building that should yield short-term gains, architecture necessarily becomes an object of consumption.

Individual works of architecture must address some of the significant challenges that Dubai will continue to face. Failure to do so will have considerable consequences for the built and natural environments. But change will occur only if building regulations, legislation, and property development practices encourage architecture and urban design that aspires to more than becoming what Arendt defined as objects of consumption. Until now, proposed projects characterized by novelty and, in some cases, parody have generated media interest and brought attention to Dubai's incredible financial success. It will be some time before it can be determined whether the proposals will meet expectations. Already extensive construction delays, unexpected problems with large-scale infrastructure improvements, and complaints about the quality of completed projects have resulted. This should not be surprising given that low-wage unskilled labor is burdened with delivering buildings that are of a standard greater than anything they may have experienced.

In progress

Dubai is not yet a paradise for architects, at least not for those concerned for the long-term implications of their work. The negotiable boundaries between government institutions, private enterprise and the elite have inspired inflows of foreign direct investment into the real-estate sector; however, the conditions that attracted investment, such as the rapid pace of development and labor conditions in the construction industry, continue to conspire against the individual work of architecture. While vast quantities of money have been invested on the basis of sales brochures, the momentum and speed that has favored speculative investment stands in stark contrast to the actual time necessary for achieving quality in design and construction. Perhaps as Dubai moves from rendering to reality, greater demands will be made by those who invest in buildings with the intention to inhabit rather than to profit.

POSTSCRIPT: PROGRESS ON PROMISES

This essay, originally written in 2006, examined the role architecture played in luring investment and promoting speculation. Characterizing Dubai as an "architect's paradise" was questionable in 2005 and, following the global financial crisis that began in late 2008, paradisiacal promises certainly proved to be illusory as individuals involved in design- and construction-related industries were part of an exodus precipitated by stalled projects. It is clear that many of the rendered representations that supported marketing efforts aimed at attracting investment will not become reality: in June 2011, Dubai's Real Estate Regulatory Agency (RERA) announced that a comprehensive review of over 450 projects resulted in the decision to cancel 217.[46]

Framing architecture in Dubai in terms of Hannah Arendt's distinction between objects of culture and objects of consumption remains useful; however, in retrospect, a more defined conceptual category is warranted. Ultimately contemporary architecture in Dubai has been treated as an object of exchange, whether in the form of speculative buildings for the purpose of rent or resale or prestige projects constructed to house cultural institutions brought from abroad. Worth is determined by the potential for profit or the possibility of enhancing status via iconic expressions or "brand recognition," not by the particular architectural qualities of buildings or contributions to creating urban spaces. Dubai and other rapidly expanding cities around the Gulf will continue to be of interest because they pose fundamental questions related to the roles of architecture and the values ascribed to the built environment.

A survey of completed projects reveals the struggle to find appropriate architectural expressions for a place that remains suspended in a state of becoming.[47] Although isolated buildings played a central role in the rush to attract investment, the promises of distinguished individual works of architecture have not been fulfilled. Unfortunately the lack of exceptional singular buildings does not result from subservience to a cohesive urban strategy but from struggles to counter the forces that have reduced works of architecture to objects of exchange.

Notes

Discussions with students in the College of Architecture, Art, and Design at the American University of Sharjah led to refinement of the chapter. The author acknowledges a debt to the late Professor Folke Nyberg. Ahmed Kanna's editorial work and efforts to make publication possible are greatly appreciated.

1 Andrew Hammond, "Futuristic Dubai—An Architect's Paradise," *San Diego Union-Tribune*, August 21, 2005.

2 Nick Tosches, "Dubai's Limit," *Vanity Fair*, June 2006, p. 156.

3 Annette Bernhardt, Laura Dresser, and Erin Hatton, "The Coffee Pot Wars: Union and Firm Restructuring of the Hotel Industry," in Eileen Applebaum, Annette Bernhardt, and Richard J. Murnane, eds., *Low-Wage America: How Employers Are Reshaping Opportunity in the Workplace* (New York: Russell Sage Foundation, 2003), pp. 33–76.

4 "Poor Salaries Leave Safety Inspectors' Posts Vacant," *Gulf News*, May 4, 2006.

5 "Al Ka'abi Proposes Two-Day Weekend for Private Sector," *Gulf News*, September 16, 2006.

6 Dubai Municipality, "Vehicles Registered for the First Time (New) and Renewed by Type–Emirate of Dubai (2002–2005)," Table Code SYB05-07-19.

7 Dubai Municipality, "Vehicles Registered in License Department by Type until End of the Year–Emirate of Dubai (2005)," Table Code SYB05-07-18.

8 Will Clift, "Green Development in the Desert," *Rocky Mountain Institute Newsletter*, Summer 2004, p. 17.

9 "Developments in the Supply and Distribution of Water in the U.A.E.," *Journal of the Emirates Industrial Bank*, vol. 19, no. 3, March 2004.

10 Dubai Municipality, *Green Area & No. of Trees & Shrubs by Type End of the Year–Emirate of Dubai (1997-2001)*, Table Code SYB01-10-08.

11 Dubai Municipality, *Green Areas and Trees by Type End of the Year–Emirate of Dubai (2001–2005)*, Table Code SYB01-10-01.

12 World Resources Institute, *EarthTrends: The Environmental Information Portal*, available at http://earthtrends.wri.org (Washington, D.C.: World Resources Institute).

13 *Country Report. United Arab Emirates* (London: The Economist Intelligence Unit Limited, 2006), p. 21.

14 International Monetary Fund, *IMF Executive Board Concludes 2005 Article IV Consultation with the United Arab Emirates*, Public Information Notice (PIN) No. 05/89, July 15, 2005.

15 Michael McDonough, "Selling Sarasota: Architecture and Propaganda in a 1920s Boom Town," *The Journal of Decorative and Propaganda Arts*, vol. 23, Florida Theme Issue (1998).

16 Mahmoud Abu-Ali, *Real Estate Market in Dubai, Variables and Numbers, Sectoral Reports 2000* (Dubai: Dubai Chamber of Commerce and Industry), p. 6.

17 Ohood Al Roumi et al., *Real Estate Sector in Dubai, Sector Monitor Series, Extended 2004* (Dubai: Dubai Chamber of Commerce and Industry), p. 21.

18 International Monetary Fund, *United Arab Emirates: Statistical Appendix*, IMF Country Report No. 06/256 (Washington, D.C.: International Monetary Fund, 2006), p. 15.

19 Gertrude Matthews Shelby, "Florida Frenzy," *Harper's Monthly Magazine*, January 1926, p. 177.

20 http://www.dubaiwaterfront.ae/au_ov.php (accessed 27 December 2006).

21 http://www.futurebrand.com/futurebrand.html (accessed 27 December 2006).

22 "Emirate Rebrands Itself as a Global Melting Pot," *Financial Times*, July 12, 2005.

23 http://www.thepalm.ae (accessed October 24, 2006).

24 Gabrielle Gwyther, "Paradise Planned: Community Formation and the Master Planned Estate," *Urban Policy and Research*, 23, 1 (2005) p. 59.

25 Andrzej Kapiszewski, *Arab versus Asian Migrant Workers in the GCC Countries*, United Nations Expert Group Meeting on International Migration and Development in the Arab Region, Beirut, May 15–17, 2006, p. 14.

26 "Springs Project not a Highway, Says Official,"*Gulf News*, February 16, 2006.

27 Hammond, "Futuristic Dubai."

28 "'Terrible' Buildings Fail to Inspire Top Designers," *Gulf News*, February 15, 2005.

29 "Britan's Top Architect Lauds Building Designs in Dubai," *Gulf News*, February 17, 2005.

30 "Guggenheim Foundation Builds its Largest Museum in Abu Dhabi," *Jerusalem Post*, http://www.jpost.com (accessed 25 October 2006).

31 Glen Osmond and Alexis Dijksterhuis, "$892 Billion FM Market," *Facilities Management Magazine-GCC Edition*, vol. 1, issue 5, p. 4.

32 Christopher Mitchell. "Development in the Middle East: The Practice of Architecture," *Bulletin (British Society for Middle Eastern Studies)*, vol. 3, 1976, p. 90.

33 Industry Canada, http://strategis.ic.gc.ca/epic/internet/inimr-ri.nsf/en/gr120252e.html (accessed 15 October 2006).

34 "Steel Quality Fears Grow as Costs Rise," *ITP Construction*, http://www.itp.net/business (accessed September 24, 2006).

35 John Fletcher, "Half of the World's Cranes Are Here," *QS Week*, January 11, 2006, p. 11.

36 "Middle East Construction Boom Will Collapse without Better Quality Concrete," *AME Info*, http://www.ameinfo.com/49153.html (accessed 15 September 2006).

37 John Willoughby, "Ambivalent Anxieties of the South Asian-Gulf Arab Labor Exchange," *Department of Economics Working Papers Series* (Washington, D.C.: American University, 2005).

38 John Urry, *The Tourist Gaze: Leisure and Travel in Contemporary Societies* (London: Sage Publications, 1990).

39 World Wildlife Fund for Nature, *Living Planet Report 2004* (Gland, Switzerland: World Wildlife Fund for Nature, 2004).

40 World Wildlife Fund for Nature, *Living Planet Report 2006* (Gland, Switzerland: World Wildlife Fund for Nature, 2006).

41 "Thermal Insulation Key to Reducing Energy Consumption," *AME Info*, http://www.ameinfo.com/84998.html (accessed September 1, 2006).

42 "The Key Word Is Savings," *Gulf News*, May 27, 2006.

43 Michael Benedikt, "Less for Less Yet: On Architecture's Value(s) in the Marketplace," *Harvard Design Magazine*, Winter/Spring 1999, p. 3.

44 United Nations Conference on Trade and Development, *World Investment Report 2006, FDI from Developing and Transition Economies: Implications for Development* (New York and Geneva: United Nations, 2006), p. 66.

45 Hannah Arendt, "The Crisis of Culture: Its Social and Cultural Significance," in *Between Past and Future* (New York: Penguin Books, 1993), pp. 197–226.

46 "Dubai Property Regulator Canceled 217 Projects in 2 Years Amid Price Slump," *Bloomberg*, http://www.bloomberg.com/news/2011-06-12/dubai-property-regulator-cancelled-217-projects-as-transactions-dry-up.html (accessed 17 June 2011).

47 Kevin Mitchell, "In What Style Should Dubai Build?" in Elizabeth Blum and Peter Neitzke, eds., *Dubai: City from Nothing* (Basel: Birkhäuser, 2009), pp. 131–140.

Contributors

Ahmed Kanna is Assistant Professor of Anthropology and International Studies at the University of the Pacific. A former Aga Khan Fellow at Harvard's Graduate School of Design, he is the author of *Dubai, The City as Corporation* (2011) and numerous essays on Arab urbanism, cultural anthropology, and the built environment. He is also the editor, with Xiangming Chen, of *Rethinking Global Urbanism* (2012). He is currently working on projects on the geographies of empire and militarism in Arab urbanism and on gentrification and discourses of sustainability in Berlin.

Amale Andraos, a principal at WORKac, received her B.Arch from McGill University in Montreal and her M.Arch from the Harvard University Graduate School of Design. She is an Assistant Professor at Columbia University's Graduate School of Architecture, Planning, and Preservation and has taught at numerous institutions including Princeton, Harvard, the University of Pennsylvania, Parsons The New School for Design, the New York Institute of Technology, and the American University in Beirut.

Gareth Doherty teaches in the departments of Landscape Architecture and Urban Planning and Design at Harvard University's Graduate School of Design. Doherty's research and teaching focus on the intersections between landscape, ecology, urbanism, and anthropology. He is a founding editor of the *New Geographies* journal at the GSD and editor-in-chief of *New Geographies 3: Urbanisms of Color* (2011). Doherty edited *Ecological Urbanism* (2010) with Mohsen Mostafavi.

Yasser Elsheshtawy is Associate Professor of Architecture at the United Arab Emirates University. His research has focused on Middle East urbanism and has resulted in numerous publications including *Dubai: Behind an Urban Spectacle*; *Planning Middle Eastern Cities*; and *The Evolving Arab City,* which won the 2010 International Planning History Society Book Prize.

Maryam Monalisa Gharavi works on visual culture, discourses of progress, and the political terrain of empire, especially in the global South. She has written on migrant labor in Dubai for the *Indian Express*. Her films have been screened at the Townhouse Gallery of Art, Pacific Film Archive, Harvard Film Archive, Women of Color Film Festival, and the Boston Palestine Film Festival, among other venues. She is a doctoral candidate in Comparative Literature and Film and Visual Studies at Harvard University.

Boris Brorman Jensen is an Associate Professor at the Aarhus School of Architecture, Denmark. He studied at the Aarhus School of Architecture, pursued graduate studies at the State University of New York in Buffalo, and earned a doctoral degree from Aalborg University. He has been a visiting academic at the University of Sydney and a guest teacher/lecturer at Chulalongkorn University in Bangkok, the KTH Royal Institute of Technology in Stockholm, and the Oslo School of Architecture and Design. He was an Aga Khan Fellow at the Harvard University Graduate School of Design.

Kevin Mitchell is an Associate Professor of Architecture in the College of Architecture, Art, and Design and currently serves as Vice Provost of Undergraduate Affairs and Instruction at the American University of Sharjah (United Arab Emirates).

Virginie Picon-Lefebvre is an architect and urban designer. She is a Professor at the Ecole Nationale Supérieure d'Architecture Paris-Malaquais and was a lecturer at the Harvard University Graduate School of Design during 2001–2007. She has a Ph.D. in Architectural History and teaches courses in urban design. She has been Professor of Architecture and Urban Design at the Ecole d'Architecture in Versailles, France, and a visiting scholar at MIT. She is the author of *La Grande Arche de la Defense* (1989) with Francois Chaslin, and the editor of *Les espaces publics modernes* (1995) and *Desert Tourism: Tracing the Fragile Edges of Development* (2011). In 1988, she founded a research group with Claude Prelorenzo, GRAI (now LIAT), to study the relationship between architecture and infrastructure.

Stephen J. Ramos is an Assistant Professor in the College of Environment and Design at the University of Georgia. He is author of *Dubai Amplified: The Engineering of a Port Geography* (2010) and co-editor of *Infrastructure Sustainability and Design* (2012). He is a founding editor of *New Geographies*. Ramos holds a Doctor of Design degree from the Harvard University Graduate School of Design.

Peter G. Rowe is the Raymond Garbe Professor of Architecture and Urban Design and University Distinguished Service Professor at the Graduate School of Design, Harvard University, where he has taught since 1985, serving as Dean from 1992 to 2004. Among his most recent publications are: *Architectural Encounters with Essence and Form in Modern China (2002)*; *Shanghai: Architecture and Urbanism for Modern China* (2004); *East-Asia Modern: Shaping the Contemporary City* (2005); *Building Barcelona: The Second Renaixença* (2006); *A City and Its Stream: The Cheonggyecheon Restoration Project* (2010); and *Emergent Architectural Territories in East Asian Cities* (2011).

Neyran Turan is an architect and an Assistant Professor of Architecture at Rice University. She is a founding editor of the Harvard University Graduate School of Design journal *New Geographies,* which focuses on contemporary issues of urbanism and architecture. Turan is also a cofounder of NEMEstudio, a research and design collaborative based in Houston. Turan received her doctoral degree from the Harvard University Graduate School of Design, and she holds a masters degree from the Yale University School of Architecture.

Dan Wood, AIA, LEED, is a principal of WORKac. He received his BA at the University of Pennsylvania and a masters degree from Columbia University. Wood is an Adjunct Professor at Princeton University's School of Architecture. He has taught at the TU Delft, the Cooper Union, Columbia University, Ohio State University, and the Berkeley School of Environmental Design, as the Friedman Distinguished Chair.